Is Jesus Still Suffering?

Is Jesus Still Suffering?

Our Power over the Heart of Jesus

Michel Esparza

Scepter

Cover image:
THE Sacred Heart OF JESUS. 2010
Oil on canvas / 30 x 24in/76 x 61cm
Artist: Stephen B. Whatley
Collection of The Carrollton School of The Sacred Heart, Miami, FL

Cover and text design by: Studio Red Design

Library of Congress Control Number: 2022909791
ISBN paperback: 978-1-59417-4674
ISBN eBook: 978-1-59417-4681

Printed in the United States of America

Contents

Introduction

The discovery that "Jesus will be in agony until the end of the world," as Pascal says, can mark a before and after in our spiritual life. This very astounding discovery, capable of turning that life upside down, can be reached by reflecting on the truth revealed by God and by diligent personal dealings with the sacred humanity of the risen Jesus Christ. It is painful to realize, however, that many Christians ignore this reality, which lends so much meaning to our relationship with God.

An anecdotal illustration: a few years ago, a priest friend of mine had to substitute for another who was attending to some people my friend hadn't known previously. Maybe that was why he decided to ask each of them: "What do you do when, without having sought it out, you meet with a setback, some sorrow or contradiction? Or if on your own initiative, you make a sacrifice or look for ways to mortify yourself: Why do you do that?" Invariably, they all responded that they would offer it up to God. Playing the devil's advocate, my intrepid friend continued his interrogation: "And what do you gain by that?" Almost all responded that they would offer it up to God for some particular intention. Many hoped it would help a child they were concerned about. Along the same lines, others explained that they were moved by the desire to obtain a physical or spiritual cure for some friend or relative. Some also claimed they would become better people for it. One said, "I hope that in heaven the Lord will make it up to me." "And what else do you gain by it?" The priest continued to insist—until they didn't know what else to say.

The responses to this little interview don't surprise me. They confirm that the last thing people who offer sacrifices or prayers to the Lord are asking themselves is *how he feels about it*. They don't put *themselves in his shoes* to find out whether it gives him (in our human way of speaking) *any pleasure or consolation*. This mindset is unfortunately very common. Right after the "I offer you" comes the "for . . ." A person gives something to the Lord, but immediately adds some concrete intention. Without any ill will, we wind up treating Jesus Christ like a mere intermediary, like an errand boy.

Unfortunately, what really moves most Christians is not so much the love of Christ as their own convenience and their love of other people. Since he is so good, this kind of conduct doesn't entirely displease him. There's no doubt that he appreciates our asking for his help, and our desire to help others. Then, too, he's aware of the ignorance, often invincible, that lies behind this way of acting. He knows that most Christians fail to be in tune with his heart because they don't realize it feels sorrow or gratitude. Nonetheless, it may be that this lack of harmony with the *sorrows and joys* of Christ's heart saddens him, especially when it's due to carelessness.

Any Christian who is diligent in prayer senses how much the way we use our freedom affects the Lord, especially if we're familiar with the lives of the saints. In particular, knowing the story of the devotion to the Sacred Heart, to which I devote a major portion of this book, is a very valuable aid. It's worth laying out this reality which most exemplary Catholics often forget about; it's worth underscoring the urgency of *consoling* someone who, since he's the one who loves the most, suffers *the* most. My concern is simply to show just how essential it is to be aware of the *joys and sorrows* the heart of Jesus experiences. If we learn how much sins hurt him, it won't be as difficult to decide to transform our life into an opportunity to ease those pains with actions that will console God the Father and obtain for us the grace of the Holy Spirit. Although the ultimate goal of this book is to foster the desire to make reparation, I've placed this in the much broader context of the Christian's spiritual life. I'm keeping in mind that affective harmony with Christ's sacred humanity is an essential aspect of our prayer life but not its final destination. Rather, it's an intermediate stage along the way toward the highest peaks of intimacy with the Father, Son, and Holy Spirit.

This book is addressed not solely to Christian believers who desire to learn to love God more, but also to those readers who may be less familiar with Catholic doctrine, but who, with an open mind, wish to draw near to the great treasures of Christian experience. Sadly, in our day, at least in the West, the religious formation of many people is clearly deficient. To make up for this lack, I address doctrinal questions and truths of faith that will help to cement the life of piety more firmly. Thus, instead of calling this book *Beyond Jesus as Errand Boy*—a title proper to a book of spirituality—this could also be called *An Introduction to the Christian's Spiritual Life*, since it enters into other aspects that lend intellectual support to the *why* of many matters, like the relation between Christ's two natures, or the origin of the *sorrow* of God. At any rate, to ensure the instructional character of these pages, I've adopted a simple terminology, more proper to preaching than to theological science. This serves the main objective of this book: that a broad audience might grasp—and *feel*, too—the urgency of making amends to the Sacred Heart of Jesus.

I hope these pages may serve, for the reader who's already convinced as well as the one who's just beginning to look into the Christian life, as a guide to solidify an intimate relationship of love with Jesus Christ who, from the Cross, invites us to spend our existence collaborating with his work of Redemption.

The first part of the book underlines the love of friendship with Christ while at the same time analyzing the means that help us most in getting to know him: the study of revealed truths and the meditative reading of the Gospel, as well as mental prayer. From there, we immerse ourselves in the captivating world of the contemplative life of union with God.

The second part centers on how we live in harmony with Jesus. In the end, the motives that move us most to joyfully *complicate* our life are two: *gratitude* for his overflowing love and *compassion* for his sorrowful heart. As with the saints, nothing stimulates our generosity so much when the time for sacrifice comes as the urge to ease the sadness of his Sacred Heart.

Logroño, Spain, February 7, 2013

Part 1

KNOWING CHRIST

Chapter 1

Friendship with Christ and its Context

Toward the Divine by Means of the Human

It's very difficult to get a precise number of the stars in the heavens. Our galaxy alone holds some hundred million stars, with twelve billion galaxies besides. I had to ask the help of an expert in astronomy to learn about these unbelievably enormous numbers. Like a good teacher, he used a comparison that simplified things greatly for me: if every star in the universe were the size of a tennis ball, he said, the earth's surface wouldn't be large enough to contain them all.

Something similar happens with inscrutable divine realities: God "dwells in unapproachable light" (1 Tm 6:16) and Christ is his "visible sign."[1] Everything divine, being

---

1   St. John Paul II, Encyclical *Dives in Misericordia* (November 30, 1980), no. 3. Vatican website: www.vatican.va.

incommensurate with what we know, is too high for us, always shrouded in mystery. Therefore revelation is so often necessary and always a cause for gratitude. Aware of our limitations, God decides to speak to us of himself. Like a good teacher, he sets up intermediate steps. In the Old Testament, he reveals himself through human metaphors: through the prophet Isaiah, for example, he tells us that he never forgets us, that he loves us more than the best of mothers (see Is 49:15).

With the Incarnation he goes much farther: he himself becomes man and reveals his own intimate life. As St. John affirms, "No one has ever seen God; the only Son, who is in the bosom of the Father, he has made him known" (Jn 1:18). Jesus Christ is, indeed, the maximum revelation of the Father. He teaches us that God is One and Triune, that in him there is at once a perfect *unity of nature* and *Trinity of Persons*: Father, Son, and Holy Spirit. Reflecting on this revealed data, we intuit that behind the unity of the Godhead is an ineffable communion of love among the divine Persons: a plenitude of Life before which what we call *life* pales.

At the same time, revelation leaves room for personal reflection in order to discover many of its truths. With the arguments of reason, for instance, we can come to know that God exists and get acquainted with some of his attributes. Contemplating the marvelous order of the universe is enough to allow us to intuit that a superior intelligence must have planned it out, just as we can't imagine software that wasn't programmed. Atoms, like bytes, are incapable of ordering themselves; they lack intelligence. Rational analysis, together with an attitude that's honest and open to reality, confirms this presentiment of the divine.

A branch of philosophy—theodicy, or natural theology—addresses all this, taking as its point of departure the classic principle that God "operates in each thing according to its own nature."[2] Just as artists leave their imprint on whatever they produce, the universe speaks to us of its Creator. Remarking on this analogy, St. John Paul II affirms that nature is like "another sacred book," which, together with the Bible, allows us to discover the beauty of God.[3]

These kinds of comparisons help us to enter into the knowledge of God and dwell on revealed mysteries. Ultimately, everything human is a point of departure for drawing near to the divine in some way. We know, besides, that God created us (Gn 1:26–27) as the first book of the Old Testament explains. Therefore, analogical reasoning allows us to formulate true propositions about God, but without understanding him fully. We can attribute to God, for instance, everything that implies perfection and excludes

2   Aquinas, *Summa Theologica*, I.83.1.3 ad 3.
3   St. John Paul II, General Audience (January 30, 2002), no. 6. Vatican website: www.vatican.va.

imperfection. It's a little like saying two men have money, although one has a dollar and the other has billions. In the same way, we can say that God is good even though we can't fully grasp his goodness.

These words of St. Augustine say it all:

> I love a certain kind of light, and sound, and fragrance, and food, and embracement in loving my God, who is the light, sound, fragrance, food, and embracement of my inner man—where that light shineth unto my soul which no place can contain, where that soundeth which time snatcheth not away, where there is a fragrance which no breeze disperseth, where there is a food which no eating can diminish, and where that clingeth which no satiety can sunder. This is what I love, when I love my God.[4]

Let's imagine that we're seeking the most suitable terms to explain that *community of love* that constitutes the Blessed Trinity. What does it mean that the Father and the Son are joined by a *bond of love* which is the Holy Spirit? When those who have contemplated the Trinitarian life try to describe the ineffable divine blessedness, they use words that are not easy to understand. They tend to allude to a *plunging* of one into the other, from which is derived a plenitude of joy

4   St. Augustine, *Confessions*, 10.6, as quoted in Vatican website: https://www.vatican.va/spirit/documents/spirit_20020903_agostino_en.html.

eternally shared. By contrast, that *embracement* allows us to intuit something of the joy that seizes both divine Persons. Even if only by contrast, it may set us thinking about how much time the longest embrace has ever lasted between a man and woman deeply in love.

Advantages of the Incarnation

The moon's light is only the sun's reflection, but the moon's lesser brilliance makes it easier to see clearly. Thus, too, in Christ, the inexpressible love of God becomes *tangible*, making our response to that love much easier. As the Spanish philosopher, García Morente, explains about his conversion,

> The distance between my poor humanity and the theoretical God of philosophy was insurmountable for me—too distant, too alien, too abstract, too geometrical and inhuman. But Christ, God made man, Christ suffering as I did, more than I did, so much more: *that was a God I could understand, and who could understand me.*[5]

5   Manuel García Morente, *El "Hecho extraordinario" y otros escritos* (Madrid: Ediciones Rialp, 1996). Editor's note: because the author has often quoted Spanish works directly or Latin works via his own translation of Latin into Spanish, rather than using English translations, this edition is often translated from the author's own text rather than that of a popular English edition. If an English edition was used in the translation process, it is noted in the citation. If the translation is directly from the author without the aid of an English version, only the Spanish or Latin text is noted.

Christ, true God and true man, loves us with his infinite divine love and with his passionate human love. Since in him there is one Person with two natures, by loving him as man we are at the same time loving God. Moreover, by taking on a human nature like our own, he makes it much easier for us to empathize and identify with the sentiments of his heart. It's not difficult to hold a conversation with Jesus in all intimacy. Without lacking in respect, we can treat him as our best friend, with greater freedom and trust, as if between equals.

It's possible to project to the supernatural plane that same affection which plays such a decisive role on the human level: it's simpler to love passionately someone who himself harbors feelings that are familiar to us. On Christmas, for instance, it's easy to be moved when contemplating the marvel of an all-powerful God who takes on the helpless, defenseless form of a little child. As St. Bernard puts it, "for the less He has made Himself in His Humanity, the greater He has been revealed in His goodness; and the more He humbles Himself on my account, the more powerfully He engages my love."[6] The Incarnation aids in the fulfillment of the most important

---

6   St. Bernard of Clairveaux, First Sermon on the Epiphany of the Lord: On the Three Manifestations of Christ, PL 43, as quoted in "St, Bernard's First Sermon for the Feast of the Epiphany," Coelifluus, January 7, 2017, https://coelifluus.wordpress.com/2017/01/07/st-bernards-first-sermon-for-the-feast-of-the-epiphany/.

commandment: to love the Lord with all our "strength" (see Mk 12:30).[7] We can employ all our resources, affective as well as spiritual, loving him not only with our head and our will but also with the madness of a heart in love.

We can never be too grateful for the Incarnation, with which Christ brings revelation to its fullness. Already preordained by God the Father in the Old Testament, the Incarnation greatly facilitates our response to his love. And there is another reason for gratitude: the Son becomes incarnate to redeem us from sin. After all, by becoming man, God takes on our own poverty-stricken condition and makes us participants in his own incomparable dignity. "For through him the holy exchange that restores our life," we pray in the liturgy, "has shone forth today in splendor: when our frailty is assumed by your Word not only does human mortality receive unending honor but by this wondrous union we, too, are made eternal."[8]

From the Earthly to the Heavenly Trinity

Christ is the best way to the Father (see Jn 14:6). He teaches us to live as good children of God and, on the Cross, he restores us to that great dignity for which we were created. Being a Father is not something *new* for God; he is Father of the Word from all eternity. The ultimate reason for his

7   See also Mt 22:37; Lk 10:27.
8   Preface 3 of Christmas.

creating us is to offer us the possibility of being *sons in the Son*. According to St. John Paul II, God "[f]irst . . . elects him, in the eternal and consubstantial Son, to participate in his sonship (through grace), and only 'after' . . . does he want creation, he wants the world, to which man belongs.[9] This *divine filiation*, by assimilating us to the Son, renders us capable of participating in the Trinitarian life. St. John, reflecting on that immense dignity, exclaims, "See what love the Father has given us, that we should be called children of God; and so we are" (1 Jn 3:1).

The divine plans for us are truly astounding; he wants to divinize us, making us "partakers of the divine nature" (2 Pt 1:4), able to know and love him eternally as he knows and loves his only begotten Son. In embryo, that divine life is already present in us from our baptism, unless we reject it through sin. We can never contemplate this blessed reality enough. It's worth doing so assiduously, since, as St. Josemaría recalls, "What a strange capacity man has to forget even the most wonderful things, to become used to mystery!"[10]

From our Lord Jesus Christ, we learn that God is a Father who desires ardently to adopt each of us. That reality shapes our entire spiritual life. Imitating Jesus leads us to conduct ourselves like the children of a Father who loves us madly.

---

9   St. John Paul II, General Audience (May 28, 1986), no. 4. Vatican website: www.vatican.va.

10   St. Josemaría Escrivá, *Christ Is Passing By* (New York: Scepter, 1974), no. 65.

We know that we're affectionately cared for like little children of the best of fathers. Knowing that he's watching out for us, always ready to forgive, floods us with peace. Someone who's not acquainted with God's goodness, when he betrays his own conscience, is annoyed to know that God is always watching. But for those who know they are children of God, that gaze makes them overflow with joy, and it helps them never to feel alone. As Benedict XVI says,

> [T]he man oriented towards love can discover in this presence that hovers everywhere a shelter for which all his being clamors. There he can overcome the sense of being alone, which no one can eliminate altogether, and which is, even so, the specific contradiction of a being that cries out for the other, for mutual accompaniment. He can find in that secret presence the foundation of the trust that allows him to live.[11]

The awareness of living under the loving gaze of God brings us gradually to acquire a genuinely contemplative life, even amid the most varied everyday matters. The heights to which we are called are thus very great indeed but not inaccessible— not when we take the hand of the best mediator, Jesus Christ. After all, even though the Christian life moves along toward

---

11 Benedict XVI, *Orar* [Prayer] (Barcelona: Editorial Planeta, 2008), p. 43.

a deep sense of *divine filiation*, it is good for it to pass *by way of diligently cultivating a relationship with Christ's sacred humanity.*

All the saints assure us that the best way to progress in the spiritual life is through the love of friendship with Jesus Christ. "In order to draw close to God," St. Josemaría reminds us, "we must take the right road, which is the Sacred Humanity of Christ."[12] Within the Church, depending on which revealed truths are accented, there are very diverse spiritualities. Some, the religious, give testimony to the transience of this world (see Mt 6:19–20), distancing themselves to a greater or lesser degree from it; others, by contrast, attend to the universal call to holiness (see Mt 5:48) from their everyday labors, striving to transform every noble human reality into an opportunity to love Christ. Moreover, all Christians have their own legitimate personal preferences. Some elements, however, are common to them all. "I can see clearly," writes St. Teresa, "that it is God's will, if we are to please Him and He is to grant us these favors, that this should be done through His most sacred Humanity, in Whom, His Majesty said, he is well pleased."[13]

---

12 St. Josemaría Escrivá, *Friends of God* (London: Scepter, 1981), no. 299. We will quote this homily of the founder of Opus Dei frequently, since I consider it the best introduction to the spiritual life of the Christian who lives in the middle of the world.

13 St. Teresa of Ávila, *The Life of Teresa of Jesus: The Autobiography of Teresa of Ávila*, ed. and trans. E. Allison Peers (n.p., n.d.), http://www.carmelitemonks. org/Vocation/teresa_life.pdf, chap. 22, p. 126.

In the path of each person, the saint declares that she doesn't interfere, but she insists that it's fitting for all of us to pass by way of Christ the man. She says this from her own experience, and corroborates it with the example of St. Paul, St. Francis of Assisi, St. Anthony of Padua, St. Bernard, and St. Catherine of Siena.

Christ is not the only intermediate link that God has placed at our disposal to draw close to him. After the heart of Jesus, the heart of Mary is the truest reflection of divine love. As St. Josemaría teaches, "*The beginning of the way*, at the end of which you will find yourself completely carried away with love for Jesus, is a confident love for Mary."[14] Jesus himself gives her to us for our mother. Baptism, by configuring us with Christ (see Rom 6:4),[15] makes us members of both his human and his divine family. As brothers and sisters of Jesus, we venerate and love Mary and Joseph. These are loves that each make the others more powerful, since each of them desires that we love the other two. With the holy Patriarch and his wife, we can have the same confidence we enjoy with our earthly parents. And, since we're Mary's children, her parents, Sts. Joachim and Anne, are our grandparents. Moreover, in Christ, we are also brothers and sisters of all the members of the *Church*, that great human and supernatural

14 St. Josemaría Escrivá, *Holy Rosary* (London: Scepter, 1987), no. 0 (Author's Note).

15 See also Gal 2:19–20; Phil 2:5.

family that unites all the children of God and Mary, whether still on earth, being purified in purgatory, or enjoying heaven. The Christian life, taken to its ultimate consequences, is demanding, like the life of a soldier in wartime, but it unfolds in that lovable and welcoming family atmosphere where we breathe the affectionate warmth of home.

Thus, along the path of the spiritual life, we go from lesser to greater. Mary leads us to Jesus, and through him, we progress to familiarity with God the Father. In its turn, that deep sense of divine filiation is the prelude to an authentic contemplative life, which brings us within the intimacy of the Blessed Trinity. From the earthly trinity, we move on to the heavenly one, establishing in the One and Triune God our permanent dwelling. The Lord wants a moment to come in which our heart remains in him like a fish in water.

The participation in the life of the Trinity is not only our definitive goal in heaven: Already here on earth, if we are faithful to our baptismal promises, the Holy Spirit lives within our soul, and with him the other Persons of the Trinity as well. If sin doesn't impede it, a sort of *umbilical cord* is established, one which attaches us to God's heart.

Referring to this wonder, Jesus says that whoever believes in him, "Out of his heart shall flow rivers of living water" (Jn 7:38). When he tries to explain the supernatural life to the Samaritan woman, he says of the Christian, "The water that I shall give him will become in him a spring of water welling up to eternal life" (Jn 4:14). With those words, he reveals to us the ineffable reality of a direct union of our soul with the *divine interiority*. With us, our *thoughts* go toward the person we love, whereas the spiritual union with God goes much farther: he establishes his dwelling in anyone who is open to his love. "If a man loves me," he says during the Last Supper, "he will keep my word, and my Father will love him, and we will come to him and make our home with him" (Jn 14:23). A little later, he says, "Abide in me" (Jn 15:40). Thus, he expresses his desire that we should learn to share in his intimacy, that we also should establish our dwelling in him. That request moves us to close our eyes often, savoring the Lord's loving presence.

Contemplating: Enlarging Our Desire

The Christian's *life of prayer* is also called the *interior life*. Since God inhabits our soul and looks upon us with love at every instant, it only makes sense to open our inner self to him. Aware of his continual solicitude for us, we can turn to him with all the confidence in the world at any moment of the day. Just as, when we're taking a solitary stroll, we find our minds teeming with all manner of thoughts, in the *presence of God* those monologues can be transformed into dialogues. For this harmony to grow, it's worth dedicating a particular time each day to prayer, to those moments of peaceful conversation with him. With time, perseverance in this habit and the inspirations of the Holy Spirit will bring us into the depths of divine intimacy. What began as a simple talk will have become deep contemplation.

In the Church's tradition, the term *contemplation* has a powerful and precise meaning. It's much more than "generically" living in the presence of God. The contemplative life consists rather of engraving indelibly on the soul's "retina" the marvelous gaze of God the Father who, in the Holy Spirit, is still in these moments loving us as sons in the Son. Contemplation tends to be associated with the word *mystical*, because it entails a *mysterious* gift of God which enables us to glimpse divine realities that far exceed our intellectual capacity by far.

These lights that God infuses in our soul allow us, for example, to contemplate the divine essence and the inter-Trinitarian life. Reading the Spanish mystics, like St. Teresa of Jesus and St. John of the Cross, or the central European ones who inspired them, like St. Gertrude and Bl. Jan van Ruusbroec, we get the impression that, each in their own way, they're all speaking of the same thing. These saints don't manage to find words to describe the ineffable, but when they try, we know that their testimony is true: we sense that they're all referring to the same reality.

When people are quick-witted, we usually say they're "full of life." There is something of this in God, but to an infinite degree. Without the "facts" that contemplation supplies, we might imagine that God is like a subdued sort of person, when in reality he is the fullness of life. Thus, while the theologians speak of the mystery of the Blessed Trinity in a rather *static* way, the mystics spot in the God who is three in one an altogether *dynamic* communion of love. For the theologians, unity in God is derived from the unity of nature (*consubstantiality*). But the saints stress the way this *unity* proceeds from the perfect loving *union* among the Father, Son, and Holy Spirit.

Let's not think that the contemplative life consists of experiencing great raptures. In general, that's not the way it works. St. Josemaría, that saint who managed to make contemplation accessible to Christians who live in the midst of temporal realities, after relating his mystical experience, adds, "I am not talking about extraordinary situations. These are, they may very well be, ordinary happenings within our soul: a loving craziness which, without any fuss or extravagance, teaches us how to suffer and how to live, because God grants us his wisdom."[16] Contemplative relations with the Lord become very simple. "Contemplation," the *Catechism* affirms, "is a *gaze* of faith, fixed on Jesus. 'I look

16   Escrivá, *Friends of God*, no. 307.

at him and he looks at me': this is what a certain peasant of
Ars in the time of his holy curé used to say while praying
before the tabernacle."[17] Mystics don't usually stress ecstasies
but the long road of interior purification that precedes the
contemplation of God.

What can we do to advance along this path of
contemplation? Above all, it's good for us to broaden our
desires. We must go deep into that innate desire that we all
harbor in the depths of our hearts. Who doesn't experience
a great eagerness for eternal happiness? Who has not, at
one time or another, identified with St. Augustine's famous
exclamation at the beginning of his *Confessions*, "You have
made us, Lord, for yourself, and our heart is restless until
it rests in you." If we're not living in a superficial manner,
that latent desire will rise to the surface, perhaps because of
some experience which recalls to us the brevity of happiness
in this life.

The *implicit* desire for God that we all harbor becomes
more *explicit* to the extent that we mature and perceive the
analogy between human and divine happiness. Noble human
love whets the appetite, but once we discover its limitations,
the desire for an unlimited love intensifies, intuited already
in this life but impossible to be realized here. If we're aware

---

17   *Catechism of the Catholic Church*, 2nd ed. Washington, DC: Libreria Editrice
Vaticana–United States Conference of Catholic Bishops, 2000, no. 2715.

of this analogy, even any simple modern song can serve as a reminder. Thus, an Irish singer expresses in one of those letters, for example, the quiet of love, something that helps to understand why in contemplative prayer words are needless.

> I never knew love could be a silence in the heart,
> A moment when the time is still;
> And all I've been looking for is right here in my arms,
> Just waiting for the chance to begin.[18]

Many are the poets who have found ways to capture in verse those profound longings of the human heart that help so much to intuit divine love. This passage of a poem by Pedro Salinas serves as an illustration: he compares passing love with the waves of the sea and counterposes it to that stable and quiet love like the water in the depths of the ocean:

> Beyond wave and foam
> desire seeks its depth.
> That depth where the sea
> made peace with its water
> and are already loving one another
> without a sign, without a movement.
> Love
> So buried in its being

---

18   "Here is Your Paradise," track 4 on Chris de Burgh, *This Way Up*, Virgin EMI, 1994.

So surrendered, so quiet
that our desire in life
is felt certain of not ending
when the kisses end
and the looks, and the signs all end
So certain of not dying
as it is
the great love of the dead.[19]

The explicit desire for God is also derived from the illuminations the Holy Spirit supplies for us. It is God himself who breaks in, allowing us to savor the unsuspected perspectives of divine love. One glimpses the "I-don't-know-what which is attained so gladly."[20] God can't be seen in this life, but all those who have, so to speak, "touched" him through a chink in this world's surface harbor an unshakable security for the rest of their days. Such a grace comes not only to great saints, like Teresa of Jesus or John of the Cross, but may be conceded to any person, even those who are living at a great distance from God.

This was the case with the French writer and journalist, André Frossard, who found faith in a surprising way when he

19   Pedro Salinas, *Razón de Amor,* verses 1184–1201, in *Poesías Completas* (Barcelona: Seix Barral, 1981), pp. 384–385.

20   "Not for all of Beauty," says St. John of the Cross, "Will I ever lose myself / But for I-don't-know-what / Which is attained so gladly." St. John of the Cross, *The Collected Works of St. John of the Cross,* trans. Kieran Kavanaugh and Otilio Rodriguez, (Washington: ICS, 1973).

visited a little chapel in Paris's Latin Quarter. He went in an atheist, as he recounts, and he came out an apostolic Roman Catholic. Besides his conversion, his experience shows that not all is joy in the contemplative life, that plenitude and emptiness go hand in hand. The fact is, someone who knows God well necessarily misses him. Frossard describes God's goodness like this: "the One whose name I can never write again without feeling the dread of wounding His tenderness, the One before whom I have the happiness of being a forgiven child, waking to learn that everything is gift."[21] After this unexpected grace, the first reaction of this formerly convinced atheist was incomprehension: Why did he have to go on living? "It did not seem at all clear to me," he relates, "why it was necessary to continue my stay on this planet when all that heaven was close enough to touch, but I accepted it out of gratitude rather than conviction."[22]

For one who has gotten a taste of the divine, not being able yet to live it in its fullness gives rise to a great heaviness. It is like the anxiousness of someone who has recently fallen in love. The contemplative is not unhappy in this world—on the contrary—but he suffers because of what St. John

21 André Frossard, *God Exists: I Have Met Him*, trans. J. F. Harwood Stevenson, accessed at "Part 3," godexists, accessed May 16, 2022, http://godexists.yolasite.com/part-3.php.

22 Frossard, *God Exists*.

of the Cross called *ausencia de figura* (absent father).[23] St. Josemaría expressed that sorrow in these terms: "We begin to live as captives, as prisoners."[24] At any rate, the solution to that problem doesn't consist in ceasing to desire but in enhancing the quality of our love, diminishing the "desire for appropriation in favor of the desire for self-giving."[25] Thus the vehement ardors of a newly enamored person give way to a more detached love in which the most important thing is for the will of the beloved to be done. When the amorous intentions are purified, those cries of "I'm dying from not dying" of earlier times are transformed into the surrendered "Your will be done!" As St. John of the Cross puts it, in the soul that has matured "will and desire are now so united in God, each in its own way, that the soul regards it as its glory that the will of God should be done in it."[26]

It's worth insisting that improving the quality of one's love for God does not entail ceasing to desire him. This would mean we had ceased to love. St. Josemaría did not

23   In his *Spiritual Canticle*, this saint says, "Reveal Your presence, / And let the vision and Your beauty kill me. / Behold the malady / Of love is incurable / Except in Your presence and before Your face." St., John of the Cross, *A Spiritual Canticle of the Soul and the Bridegroom Christ*, ed. Benedict Zimmerman, OCD, trans. David Lewis (n.p., 1909), stanza 11, electronic edition with modernization of English by Harry Plantinga, 1995, at Christian Classics Ethereal Library, https://www.ccel.org/ccel/john_cross/canticle.xvii.html.

24   Escrivá, *Friends of God*, no. 296.

25   Maria Isabel Alvira, *Vision de l'homme selon Thérèse d'Avila* (Paris: F.X.Guibert/O.E.I.L., 1992), p. 363.

26   St. John of the Cross, *Living Flame of Love,* explanation of stanza 1, no. 23.

sympathize with the sentiment "I'm dying from not dying," since he underlined being available to struggle on earth for as many years as the Lord might wish. Still, in the last years of his life, he was "dying" to see the Lord. With the words of a psalm, he kept on repeating, "Thy face, LORD, do I seek" (Ps 27:8).[27]

---

27   The Latin text says, "Vultum tuum, Domine, requiram!"

Chapter 2

Son of God and Son of Mary

With the Head and the Heart

Since Christ is the way to the highest contemplation of the divine life, it's worth exploring how we can draw close to him. To know him in an objective way, we have available the truths of revelation, offered to us through reading the *Gospel* and studying *Christian doctrine*. And in a later and parallel sequence, we draw closer and know him more intimately through *prayer*. In this way, doctrine and life go hand in hand and allow us to know Christ with both head and heart. Faith illumines the intelligence, allowing it to know God's love. As a consequence, the will is strengthened, and the heart ignited.

In order to progress adequately along this path, reflection and experience must play balanced roles. On the one hand, a person with advanced theology degrees who neglects prayer

and the sacraments wouldn't get very far, because the depths
to revealed truths are only revealed when they're lived out.
For instance, Vittorio Messori, the Italian journalist and
writer, recalls, "[T]o those who asked him who he was,
Jesus didn't distribute pamphlets or theology treatises but
proposed to them a concrete, tangible, and visual experience:
'Come and see.' "[1]

On the other hand, experience needs an objective
counterpoint. Whoever prays, yet neglects religious
formation, runs the risk of remaining trapped in a fantasy.
It's true that God will come to the aid of someone who hasn't
been able to receive any formation, but the ordinary way is
to begin with the *Catechism*. God is able to give us the light
needed to comprehend supernatural mysteries. Think of
the *theophany* André Frossard experienced. But these private
inspirations, being filtered through a person's subjectivity,
offer less certitude. Along the same lines, it's a fact that the
most magnificent mystical experience of one person can leave
another, who doesn't want to believe, indifferent.[2]

Because of our hunger for God, spirituality will always be
in style. Sadly, the same can't be said of objective revelation,

1   Vittorio Messori, *Por qué creo: Una vida para dar razón de la fe* [Why I believe],
    2nd ed. (Madrid: Libros Libres, 2009), p. 120. Translation our own.
2   Thus, we can understand, for example, the atheism of Jean Baruzi, one of
    the most authoritative experts on St. John of the Cross. See H. Arts, *Ein
    Kluizenator in New York* (Amberes: De Niederlandsche Boekhandel, 1986),
    p. 119.

with all its moral implications. With the excuse of fighting
religious intolerance and promoting spiritual freedom, not a
few Christians have succumbed to the apparent enchantments
of syncretistic viewpoints of an eastern style, such as New
Age beliefs. If followed through, these dispense with God
and reduce prayer to a simple technique of mental relaxation.
For this reason, it's worth insisting that "Christian prayer is
always determined by the structure of the Christian faith,
in which the very truth of God and creature shines forth."[3]

Many everyday examples can show the importance of a
thorough knowledge of the truths revealed by Christ. Not
long ago, a friend recounted an anecdote that was quite
enlightening. He was walking in London and wanted to
go into a church to pray before the Blessed Sacrament in
the tabernacle. The question was how to tell whether the
church he was approaching was Catholic or Protestant. The
difference is crucial, precisely because of the Real Presence
of Jesus Christ in the Eucharist. My friend would usually
look at the schedules at the entrances. If they announced
"services," it was Protestant, whereas if they referred to
"Masses," it was Catholic. During these investigations, a
friendly Anglican lady approached him to ask if he wanted
anything and invited him to enter. My friend explained to

3   Congregation for the Doctrine of the Faith, Letter on Some Aspects of
     Christian Meditation *Orationis Formas* (October 15, 1989), no. 3. Vatican
     website: www.vatican.va.

her that he was Catholic, and so he knew he wouldn't be encountering the Lord in the tabernacle. Startled, the good Anglican woman replied, "But Jesus is everywhere!" He tried to explain—in vain, I'm afraid—that Christ, as God, is indeed everywhere but that his sacramental presence in the Eucharist is another, much nearer presence, which was only possible because of the Incarnation.

This anecdote illustrates the extent to which the truths of faith shape lived experience. Protestants, not knowing about the Real Presence of Jesus Christ in the Eucharist, cannot enjoy this great gift of love of having him near us, hidden but alive. Where his Body is, there we encounter also his soul and divinity. Thus the importance of knowing all the truths revealed by God. Specifically, if we're not familiar with the "full significance of Christ's Incarnation,"[4] the Christian life suffers: it becomes "spiritualist."

Since religious theory and practice each have a claim on the other, we will study them both equally. Later, we'll go into the importance of personal dealings with the Lord by means of prayer. But first, we need to delve into Christology: that branch of theology which is concerned with analyzing the objective data revealed by God about the mystery of Christ.

4   Escrivá, *Friends of God*, no. 74.

True God

Twenty-one centuries ago, the Word, the Second Person of the Blessed Trinity, was made flesh. Ever since then, as Benedict XVI states, "[n]ow the word is not simply audible; not only does it have a *voice*, now the word has a *face*, one which we can see: that of Jesus of Nazareth."[5] To the eyes of faith, the Incarnation is the most important fact of history.

Christianity is the only religion whose founder claims to be God. Early on, the most elementary prudence led him to express it in a veiled manner to ward against a wrathful reaction among the Jews (see Jn 8:24, 28, 58). Let's not forget that he was killed for making himself equal to God (see Mt 26:64).[6] This message, however, grew more and more pointed and at the end of his life he asserted it forcefully: "I and the Father are one" (Jn 10:30). His interlocutors' response leaves no room for equivocations: they wanted to stone him as a blasphemer who was making himself equal to God (see Jn 10:33). The most explicit affirmation of his divinity was at the Last Supper: "If you had known me, you would have known my Father also; henceforth you know him and have seen him." "He who has seen me has seen the Father" (Jn 14:7, 9).

---

5   Benedict XVI, Apostolic Exhortation on the Word of God in the Life and Mission of the Church *Verbum Domini* (September 30, 2010), no. 12. Vatican website: www.vatican.va.

6   See also Mk 14:62.

Christ's divinity constitutes the foundation of Christianity's truth. If Christ is God, the religion he founded is necessarily the true one. It doesn't originate in outlandish claims or subjective experiences, but from the initiative of the one God who, becoming incarnate, has made himself visible, palpable (see Jn 1:18).[7] In contrast to what happens in other religions, supported by the testimony of a man—Mohammed, for instance, in the case of the Muslims—the Christian only trusts in the one who assures us that he is God. If we believe him, we accept likewise all that he has taught us, whether it's the Eucharist or matters pertaining to eternal life. If he has revealed a hundred truths to us, the most reasonable thing is to believe them, even before knowing what they are. We don't assent because we understand them—among these truths are also mysteries that exceed our intelligence—but because the only one who can neither deceive nor be deceived affirms them. As St. Josemaría observes, when considering these truths of faith, we realize "the limitations of our minds and the greatness of revelation. Yet even if we cannot fully grasp these truths that overawe our reason, we believe them humbly and firmly. Backed by the testimony of Christ, we know they are true."[8]

7   See also 1 Jn 1:1.
8   Escrivá, *Christ Is Passing By*, no. 169.

If all faith depends upon Christ's divinity, let us see now why it is reasonable to believe in it. He himself, when he affirms it, points us to his works (see Jn 10:38; 14:11). His miracles, indeed, confirm his word. And those who relate them are trustworthy (see Lk 1–4), perfectly sensible people who would rather die than deny what they have *seen and heard*.[9] When the Jewish authorities forbid Peter and John to "speak or teach at all in the name of Jesus," they answer: "Whether it is right in the sight of God to listen to you rather than to God, you must judge; for we cannot but speak of what we have seen and heard" (Acts 4:18–20). What they're handing on to us, then, are not complicated theories but something simple that anybody can understand: that they have seen someone who said he was God and worked all kinds of miracles. If someone claims to be God, there are three possibilities: he's mad, or he's deceiving us, or he's telling the truth. The historical witnesses corroborate that in Christ the first two possibilities can be excluded.

No contemporary of Jesus doubted that he was really a man—it was obvious—but he claimed categorically something that the senses don't perceive and only faith can accept: that he was, at the same time, God. Faith is a divine gift that

---

9   His last miracle was his own glorious Resurrection; see Mt 28; Mk 16;
     Lk 24; and Jn 20–21.

requires both evangelization[10] and good will. If we make clear that believing in Christ is the most reasonable thing, it's easier for the free will of the hearer to adhere to the truth that's been announced, but even the best preaching doesn't lead automatically to faith; not even witnessing miracles can guarantee anything if a good disposition is lacking.[11] The apostle Thomas believed in Jesus Christ's divinity after confirming the miracle of his Resurrection (see Jn 20:26-28), but that was because he freely predisposed himself to receive the gift of faith. As St. John Paul II observes, "regardless of how much his body was seen or touched, *only faith could fully enter the mystery of that face.*"[12]

Due to prejudices, attempts to discredit Christ's divinity have not been lacking. To this end, since the nineteenth century, certain authors began to cast doubt upon the historicity of the Gospels. It's not that they offer proofs; they just manage to sow doubt. It has cost more than a century of scientific work on the part of experts in exegesis and archeology to refute these unfounded doubts. Today we know that some five thousand manuscripts of the New

10 St. Paul asks, "How are they to believe in him of whom they have never heard? And how are they to hear without a preacher?" (Rom 10:14).

11 The best example is, perhaps, the reaction of the Pharisees to the resurrection of Lazarus (Jn. 11:45–53).

12 St. John Paul II, Apostolic Letter at the Close of the Great Jubilee of the Year 2000 *Novo Millennio Ineunte* (January 6, 2001), no. 19. Vatican website: www.vatican.va.

Testament have been preserved, some of which date back to the second and third centuries. The differences between them are minimal and only pertain to secondary details. Their historical reliability is greater than that of the classical Greek and Latin writers, whose oldest copies are scarce and separated from the originals by more than a thousand years. In Plato's case, for example, the separation is thirteen centuries. The same is true of the Latin classics. Ronald Knox pointed out that "we have full manuscripts of the New Testament which go back to the fourth century, whereas our oldest MS of Tacitus, for example, about the same period of writing, only dates from the ninth century."[13]

One Person and Two Natures

Adhering to the Faith doesn't prevent us from wondering how Jesus Christ can be at the same time God and man. The Incarnation is a mystery, but we can always dig deeper into its content. One of the first to do so was St. Paul, who affirmed that in Christ "the whole fulness of deity dwells bodily" (Col 2:9). In him, the divine lies hidden "behind" the human. God doesn't disguise himself as a man: he truly became man. And he will continue to be a man in heaven

---

13   Ronald A. Knox, *The Hidden Stream: Mysteries of the Christian Faith* (San Francisco: Ignatius, 2003), p. 81.

for all eternity, since "Christ bears with him his transfigured corporeality until life eternal."[14]

It's worth underscoring the importance of this *permanent character of the Incarnation*. By making himself man, God breaks into our history: "Time itself is now pervaded by eternity."[15] On the other hand, since the Ascension of Jesus Christ into heaven, "the human condition has been permanently linked to divinity,"[16] since his most holy humanity, transfigured but not dehumanized, has penetrated to the very intimacy of the eternal Godhead. Thus, God didn't just share our history twenty-one centuries ago; the Incarnation is still fully ongoing! The fact that God, in Christ, has made himself accessible to all Christians of all eras means a definitive step forward in our relations with him. Although we don't see Jesus now, we can treat him like a contemporary, with the same familiarity with which his first disciples treated him, the way we'd treat a brother or a best friend.

Let's analyze the revealed data on the mystery of the Incarnation.[17] These are basically clear: Jesus Christ is true God and true man; in him there is a *unity* of Person (a single

14 Romano Guardini, *Nur wer Gott kennt, kennt den Menschen* (Only he who knows God knows man), booklet, January 1952.

15 St. John Paul II, General Audience (December 10, 1997). Vatican website: www.vatican.va.

16 Julian Marías, *La perspectiva cristiana* (Madrid: Alianza, 1999), pp. 63–64.

17 See *Catechism*, nos. 456–483. For another investigation the following theology manual may be useful: F. Ocáriz, L. F. Mateo-Seco, J. A. Riestra, *El Misterio de Jesucristo*, 3rd ed. (Pamplona: EUNSA, 2004).

"I," subject, or individual) and a *duality* of natures: he is *one* (divine) Person who underpins the existence of *two* natures (human and divine).[18] The Church's magisterium arrived at this conclusion, threading its way between heresies that threw into doubt some of these revealed truths. Various ecumenical councils formulated with increasing precision the basis of this mystery.[19] Thanks to the assistance of the Holy Spirit, we know for a certainty that Jesus Christ is no *less* God for having become man, nor *less* man for being God. Now, as from all eternity, Christ continues to be the Second Person of the Blessed Trinity of the same divine nature as the Father (*consubstantial*) beyond all space and time. Moreover, for twenty centuries, the Person of the Word has taken on an integral human nature, becoming like us "in all things but sin" (Heb 4:15). Our Lord Jesus Christ is, then, perfect God and perfect man.

18   That union of two natures in a single person is called the *hypostatic union* (*hipóstasis* means person).

19   The Council of Nicea (325) and the First Council of Constantinople (381) drew attention to the divinity of Christ, refuting *Arianism,* which denied Christ's divinity, and *Nestorianism*, which held that in Christ a human person was also present. Later, the Council of Ephesus (431) defined the hypostatic union (two natures united in the Person of the Word). For its part, the Council of Chalcedon (451) clarified the relationship between the two natures and condemned the heresy of *monophysitism*, which cast doubt on the true humanity of Christ. Everything became still clearer in the Second Council of Constantinople (553). Finally, the Third Council of Constantinople drew out the consequences of the earlier ones and, against *monothelitism*, affirmed that in Christ there are two wills, two intelligences, and, therefore, two kinds of operations.

The fifth-century Council of Chalcedon defined that the two natures of Christ are joined "without confusion, without change, without division, and without separation."[20] In other words, his humanity and his divinity are united "without mixture or division."[21] From such a union, we see that Jesus Christ is neither less God nor less man. The terms *without confusion* and *without mixture* entail relevant practical consequences. Given that his human nature is in no way negated by the divine one, without forgetting that he is God, we can treat him as if he were only man.

It's not a question, then, of the divine and the human being all mixed up together. The Word took on human nature without absorbing it.[22] It's as if a little bit of oil were to fall into an enormous container of water: no matter how much we might shake them up, the two liquids don't mix. The lack of empathy that many Christians feel for Christ's sacred humanity is due, in practice, to the way they fail to see him as true man. They imagine him as if he were some sort of human-divine *hybrid*.

It's also worth noting that the Church's doctrine, holding true to the duality of nature, affirms that in Christ there are two wills, two intelligences, and, therefore, two types of

---

20 "*Inconfuse, inmutabiliter, indivise et inseparabiliter,*" says the original text.

21 Divine Office, Lauds of January 1, antiphon "*Ad benedictus.*"

22 "*Assumpta sed non absorpta.*" See St. Paul VI, Pastoral Constitution on the Church in the Modern World *Gaudium et Spes* (December 7, 1965), no. 22.

operations: one divine and one human. The two wills give rise to two ways of loving: one divine and one human. As man, he harbors a perfect love, but it doesn't cease to be genuinely human. The love of the sacred humanity of Christ is the most faithful reflection of divine love, but it doesn't stop being a human love that brings with it feelings like our own.

A Heart of Flesh Like Our Own

With the expression *Sacred Heart of Jesus*, we refer to an area much broader than the merely sentimental. The term *heart* indicates the center of the affective sphere, not only what we feel, but also the ultimate ground of our interiority.[23] "When we speak of a person's heart, we refer not just to his sentiments, but to the whole person in his loving dealings with others."[24] Thus, considering the *unity of persons* in Christ, we can truly affirm that his heart is the *point* at which his human love and his divine love come together.[25] This means that the Person of the Word loves by means of human affections. In him, the divine pulses behind the human and perfects it to its highest point. Thus, we understand expressions like this one of St. Josemaría: "Christ loves us with all the inexhaustible charity of God's own heart."[26]

23   See *Catechism*, no. 2563.
24   Escrivá, *Christ Is Passing By*, no. 164.
25   "Heart of Jesus in whom there dwells the fullness of God," says the Litany to the Sacred Heart.
26   Escrivá, *Christ Is Passing By*, no. 59.

But let us not forget the other part of the mystery: the *duality of natures*. That all of God is loving through the use of a perfect human heart doesn't mean that it ceases to be a heart of flesh like our own. The Old Testament, to make divine things accessible to us, talks to us of God's love with passionate language.[27] In a strict sense, though, however noble and upright affective passion may be, it can't be attributed to God but only to the human person. The Faith tells us that in Christ there are two intelligences and two wills, but not two hearts or two souls. As Dietrich von Hildebrand points out, "we are touching on the deepest and noblest mark of human nature, to have a heart capable of love, a heart which can know anxiety and sorrow, which can be afflicted and moved, is the most specific characteristic of the human person."[28]

In Christ, the human reflects the divine but does not exhaust it. A human heart, no matter how perfect, is nonetheless limited, so that it cannot fully express the immensity of divine love. We could say that Christ's human love is the most faithful—though reduced—copy of his divine love. His heart of flesh is the most perfect one ever to have existed, but it doesn't cease to be authentically human. His affections possess an unparalleled uprightness, but they do not thereby cease to be genuinely passionate.

27 See, for example, Song 5:2; Prv 7:3; also Ps 12:6; 21:15; 39:9; 44:2; 56:8.
28 Dietrich von Hildebrand, *The Heart: An Analysis of Human and Divine Affectivity* (South Bend, IN: St. Augustine's Press, 2007), p. 203.

Once again: in Christ, the human is no less human by
virtue of his being God, nor the divine any less divine for
having been made man.

  Thus, it's not easy to *speak of Christ with theological precision*,
since in him are present two realities difficult to reconcile:
the unity of person and diversity of natures. If one or the
other receives undue emphasis, we get the impression that
there are two persons, or a single nature. On the one hand
are those who focus on his humanity to the detriment of
his divinity. These *new Arians* talk so much about "Jesus of
Nazareth" that they seem not to believe that he's God at
all. They talk about him as if he were on the same plane of
importance as Socrates or other historical figures whom we
admire for their integrity.

  This reflects, at bottom, a major problem of faith, since
denying Christ's divinity is equivalent to destroying the
foundation of the Christian religion. On the other hand,
there are those who draw so much attention to the divine
that they nearly deny his humanity. For fear of lacking in
the respect due to the Son of God, they do not altogether
take in the *depth of the Incarnation*. Thus, the concern with
safeguarding Jesus' divinity and holiness above all, joined
to a certain tendency to idealize, can bring them to view
him as less human than he really is. Even if they do not in
theory cast doubt on his human nature, this nature does

imperceptibly, in practice, wind up being eclipsed by his divine dignity.[29] Thus the insistence with which, in these pages, we draw attention to the human vessel of Christ's love, taking for granted his divinity.

That doctrinal clarity is a great help in our dealings with the Lord. Consequently, with the soul of a little child, the heart expands easily when contemplating Jesus in the crib of Bethlehem, without forgetting that this Child is the King of the Universe. This familiar way of relating to Christ the man doesn't prevent our recalling his infinite divine dignity. If, for example, we're contemplating Christ being insulted during the Passion, we recall that he's still the Son of God, that behind his humanity lies his divinity. During his earthly life, except on a very few occasions—like his transfiguration on Mount Tabor—Christ doesn't allow his divinity to be visibly observable by means of his body. This doesn't happen now that he is glorified in heaven.

Everything affirmed about the dignity of Christ is also applicable to Mary, although on a different level. With her, something similar comes into play to what happens with Christ's two natures. Since she's our mother, we can treat her with full filial confidence. But this familiarity should not lead us to forget the veneration she deserves as Mother of God. She

29   The error into which these well-intentioned Christians inadvertently fall could be called *practical monophysitism*.

is the mother of Christ the man and, since he is at the same time God, she is truly the Mother of God (though not of his divinity), the door through which Christ came into the world. The more astonished we are before the Incarnation, the better we will understand the Marian privileges. Words fall short for expressing the dignity of the Most Holy Mother, daughter of God the Father, Mother of God the Son, spouse of God the Holy Spirit. Nevertheless, in practice, without forgetting that she is *queen*, our filial affection brings us to see her above all as *Mother of Mercy*.

Chapter 3

The Perfect Man in the Gospel

Christ's Personality

Jesus Christ's perfection doesn't mean that God was made "man in general," but *one* man in particular. He was a man, not a woman; he has an unrepeatable history and a particular personality. Two human beings can be equally perfect yet have very different characters. For this reason, to foster empathy with *that man*, we need the greatest possible amount of information about his way of being.

Since we still can't see him (though he can see us), we want to know his interiority, and know it now. The fonder we grow of him, the more we desire to get to know his personality. The Gospel is the best place to meet him. To meditate fruitfully, at the same time as we converse with the Lord, it makes sense for us to delve into each one of the scenes. The evangelists, concerned above all with historical rigor, tend to be quite sparing when it's time to relate the concrete circumstances surrounding the events, limiting themselves to relating the words pronounced by Jesus. Thus the importance of our imagining what they omit.

When we meditate on the Gospel, we are learning to imitate the Master. Here is an outline of his proven personality. "He preached and taught with authority. He was humiliated, or, rather, they humiliated him, and he was patient; he condescended without cheapening himself; he gave himself up with total resignation but did not forfeit his superiority; he gave, but he did not impose himself or crush anyone."[1] Aware of his own dignity, Jesus knew how to combine what is so difficult for us: *dependence on* and *independence of others*. He offered himself up without reserve but with full interior freedom. Therefore, by means of his example, we discover our most profound truth. St. John Paul II never tired of insisting on this. It is "God who comes in Person," he said in 1998, "to speak to man of himself and to show him the path by which he may be reached"[2] This is not

1   Jose Maria Pich, *El Cristo de la Tierra*, 3rd ed. (Madrid: Ediciones Rialp, 1974,) p. 36.
2   St. John Paul II, Apostolic Letter on Preparation for the Jubilee of the Year 2000 *Tertio Millennio Adveniente* (November 10, 1994), no. 6. Vatican website: www.vatican.va. See also St. Paul VI, *Gaudium et Spes*, no. 22.

the moment to analyze each one of Christ's virtues. To use one example, let us focus simply on his great capacity to love.

A Capacity to Grow with the Heart of Christ

Jesus Christ has none of that pride which causes the self-obsessed emotions or feelings that we experience on account of original sin. Unlike his creatures, Jesus' heart harbors no egotistical need, nor does it require it. Instead, his divine nature elevates to the supernatural, the sentiments of ordinary human nature to which his divine nature is united. These sentiments have no limits, and so they show a new and higher dimension of the heart. Von Hildebrand explains that

> a transfigured affectivity permeates Christian morality. It is an affectivity that differs fundamentally from any natural affectivity. But this difference does not consist in less ardor, less tenderness, less affectivity. On the contrary, it is a limitless affectivity, one which discloses new and unheard-of dimensions of the heart.[3]

In the Gospels, we see that Jesus Christ avoids both *sentimentalism* and *insensibility*. His affectivity, or inclination, is exempt from any egotism or superficiality. His affections are detached, but not any less intense than ours for that reason. His great capacity for love is manifest in a myriad of

3   Hildebrand, *The Heart*, p. 209.

details: he embraces the children (see Mk 9:36); he is moved each time that he meets with suffering people (see Mt 9:2; 9:36);[4] he loves his friends[5]—thus his deep sadness upon the death of Lazarus (see Jn 11:33–35, 38); he says he is "meek and humble of heart" (Mt 11:29);[6] he looks with affection on the young rich man (see Mk 10:17-31); and he is concerned for his disciples to be able to relax in a family atmosphere (see Mk 6:31).

After the Resurrection, we observe the same sentiments: he addresses Mary Magdalen in a tone that betrays his emotion (see Jn 20:15-16) and shows his concern for the disciples' fishing success (see Jn 21:5); to the disciples on the road to Emmaus, he speaks passionately (see Lk 24:25–26). The conversation with Peter by the Sea of Tiberius, where he asks him three times if he loves him (see Jn 21:15–19) shows the affection with which Jesus continues to regard him, as well as his desire to be responded to with all affection and devotion.

From Jesus we learn to be affectionate but not soft, detached but not indifferent. Thus, we avoid the false spiritualities that dehumanize us as well as the excesses of an unbridled affection. As St. Josemaría states, if we despise the affective,

4   See also Mk 6:34; Lk 7:13.
5   "Jesus loved Martha and her sister and Lazarus" (Jn 11:5).
6   NABRE translation.

[w]e would [be] capable only of an "official charity," dry and soulless . . . . Not the true charity of Jesus, which involves affection and human warmth. In saying this, I am not supporting the mistaken theories—pitiful excuses—which misdirect hearts away from God and lead them into occasions of sin and perdition."[7]

In the end, the moral value of the passions depends on what use we make of them. "Emotions and feelings can be taken up into the virtues or perverted by the *vices*."[8] It's not a question of repressing the affections but of purifying them, trying to remove from them the imprint of egotism and irrationality. At bottom, this positive attitude toward the noble human realities derives from the Incarnation. Jesus is the master of humanity, something that is not well understood by those who don't understand "the full significance of Christ's Incarnation."[9]

Christ also teaches us to bring together all the resources available to us, whether affective, intellectual, or volitive. What's needed is addition, not subtraction: the ideal person combines the clear mind of an engineer, the strong will of an athlete, and the ardent heart of a poet. Moreover, these all move forward parallel to each other, mutually supporting each other so that

---

7   Escrivá, *Christ Is Passing By*, no. 167.

8   *Catechism*, no. 1768.

9   Escrivá, *Friends of God*, no. 74.

the person grows harmoniously. Otherwise, instead of helping each other, they get in each other's way. The heart can aid the intellect and the will, but if it gets out of line, leaving its natural role behind, as with *sentimentalism*, it disturbs the activity of the spiritual potencies. For their part, if the intellect and the will are frittered away, a person can fall easily into *intellectualism* or *voluntarism*, attitudes in which the heart counts for nothing. To avoid these three deformations, "the intellect, the will, and the heart should cooperate, but each must respect the specific role and domain of the other. The intellect or will should not try to supply what only the heart can give, nor should the heart arrogate the role of the intellect or will."[10]

Like a two-edged sword, the heart presents two *advantages* and two *disadvantages*: with regard to the intellect, it sharpens ingenuity and blinds reason; with respect to the will, it facilitates generosity and makes detachment difficult. We can get quite a precise idea of the sentiments of Jesus' heart by analyzing our own, removing what is negative and increasing what's positive. The Gospels corroborate that Jesus possesses all the advantages of affectivity and none of the drawbacks. Getting to know the feelings of his heart opens up for us consoling perspectives of *reciprocal affective harmony*. When two hearts beat in unison, sharing joys and sorrows, both benefit: the joys of each intensify; the sorrows lighten.

10   Hildebrand, *The Heart,* p. 98.

A Merciful Heart

Affection, put at the service of the intellect, eases the way for this *empathy*, which in turn goes such a long way toward fostering compassion for the needs of others. The Gospel accounts highlight Jesus' great capacity to feel compassion for the misery of others. When he arrived at Nain, for example, where a young man was being buried, "the only son of his mother, and she was a widow," the Lord, upon seeing her, had compassion on her, and told her, "Do not weep" (Lk 7:12–13). His compassion led him to make an exception: he raised the son without even asking for any sign of faith from his mother. The miracle was a "sign of the power of Christ who is God. But first came his compassion, an evident sign of the tenderness of the heart of Christ the man."[11]

Jesus' heart is in fact *compassionate* and *merciful*. The Gospel recounts, "When he saw the crowds, he had compassion for them, because they were harassed and helpless, like sheep without a shepherd" (Mt 9:36). He feels the wretchedness of others as his own; this is why he suffers so much and is ready to place every means of alleviating it within their reach. This also explains his preaching on behalf of the neediest, especially sinners (see Mt. 9:12). The Gospel offers us abundant material for imagining his merciful countenance. His gaze upon Levi, Zacchaeus, the woman caught in adultery, the

11   Escrivá, *Christ Is Passing By*, no. 166.

thief, the Samaritan woman, and in a special way, Peter (Mk 2:13–17),[12] is no severe look of recrimination. It reveals, instead, the eagerness to be reconciled with his lost friend. It's an irresistible mixture of tender compassion and loving reproach; it expresses—at the same time and for the same reason—love: sorrow for the offense and the desire to make peace; pain that it tries to hide and the hope of a happy outcome.

His affection leads Jesus to be concerned for each person in particular. Thus, during the Last Supper, his heart is saddened at the thought of Judas. He's on the point of performing actions of extraordinary transcendence, like the institution of the Eucharist and the Passion, but he interrupts his discourse several times to refer to the disciple who is going to betray him. He is going to consummate the Redemption of the human race, and he's concerned for the salvation of the unfaithful disciple.[13] Isn't that paradoxical? But he doesn't let himself be led by the irrationality of the heart. He knows how to take care of large

12   See also Lk 19:1–10; 22:61; 23:39–43; Jn 4:1–30; 8:1–11.

13   That great interior sorrow of Jesus because of a single sin shows us that it is not possible, as has sometimes been suggested, that a little later, in the Garden of Olives, he could suffer for each and every one of the sins that would be committed until the end of the world. That idea suffers from "practical monophysitism," because it weakens the imperatives of Christ's humanity. With attention to his divinity, the *Catechism* can affirm that "Jesus knew and loved us each and all during his life, his agony and his Passion, and gave himself up for each one of us: 'The Son of God . . . loved me and gave himself for me' [Gal 2:20]" (*Catechism*, no. 478). In Gethsemane, Christ, as God, knew the future, but as man he could not suffer so much in so little time. He suffered as much as was humanly possible at that time.

matters without neglecting smaller ones. He's not maudlin, like a man who, for fear of grieving someone, doesn't dare to speak truths that are painful but helpful.

In tandem, the gospel contains powerful admonitions for those who put their eternal salvation at risk. Thus, when he announces to his disciples for the first time that he has come to suffer, Peter rebels. He doesn't understand because he's thinking only with his heart. So, moved by an all-too-human affection, he tries to dissuade Jesus from going to Jerusalem. The Lord reproaches him harshly: "[Y]ou are not on the side of God, but of men" (Mt 16:23).

Christ's tough warnings—with the Pharisees or defending the honor of his Father when expelling the moneychangers from the temple (see Jn 2:13–22)—are not inspired by that rage which blinds the reason. His *righteous indignation* contrasts with that irascible conduct that proceeds from wounded pride. "Jesus," comments St. Josemaría, "is never distant or aloof, although sometimes in his preaching he seems very sad, because he is hurt by the evil men do. However, if we watch him closely, we will note immediately that his anger comes from love."[14] There is no "touchiness" in him. Thus, sins and ingratitude hurt him a lot, but they don't anger him.

Jesus suffers to the extent that he loves us: the immensity of his sorrow is directly proportionate to the intensity

---

14   Escrivá, *Christ Is Passing By*, no. 162.

of his affection. Fortunately, the heart involves not only vulnerability but also the ability to rejoice. So it is that the joy we obtain for the Lord is also multiplied in the measure of his love for us. A little detail of affection produces for him a joy perhaps a hundred times greater than ours would be under the same circumstances. Between his feelings and our own there is a difference not only in intensity but also in quality. His warmth is the most beautiful that has ever existed, because it's not contaminated by egotism: there's no vanity in his joys, and his sufferings have nothing to do with wounded pride. He rejoices and suffers simply because he loves. Coldness only makes him suffer because he sees his desire to contribute to our happiness thwarted.

Perhaps the more we've gone on describing the feelings of Christ, the more we've realized the imperfections of our own. Still, far from becoming discouraged, we can have recourse to him and, as in the litanies to the Sacred Heart, tell him, "Make our hearts like your own!"[15] We have hope, since the love of his heart can purify ours. Jesus Christ is not only a *model* of humanity; he is also the *source* of a grace that capacitates us to love as he does. "The love of Christ," says St. John Paul II, "makes man worthy to be loved. Created in the image and likeness of God, man has received a heart that desires to love and is capable of doing so. The love of

15   See United States Conference of Catholic Bishops, *Litany of the Sacred Heart of Jesus*, https://www.usccb.org/prayers/litany-sacred-heart-jesus.

the Redeemer, which cures the wound of his sin, elevates him to the dignity of a son."[16] That sanctifying grace that heals us and dignifies us arrives mainly by means of the *sacraments*, especially baptism, reconciliation (confession), and the Eucharist.

If we still harbor any doubts about our possibilities of sanctification, let us rely on the solicitude of our mother. Because she is *full of grace*, her heart most resembles Jesus' own. No other creature will ever cultivate such intense, disinterested, and detached affection as the Maid of Nazareth. Her holiness constitutes for us a firm reason for hope. Indeed, if the heart of a creature like Mary, with the grace of God and her own good will, could be transformed to such a degree, what will happen with us if we humbly permit the grace of God to purify our own hearts?

From Mary we learn that humility. With the *Magnificat* (Lk 1:46–56), she instructs us in this disconcerting evangelical logic which leads us to make good use even of our weakness. In her, the *maternally merciful face* of God the Father draws closer to us. If we go astray, her evident maternal compassion subdues our pride and recalls to us her Son's unconditional love. There is a reason that St. Josemaría observed, "We go to Jesus—and we 'return' to him—through Mary."[17]

---

16 St. John Paul II to Msgr. Raymond Séguy, bishop of Autun, June 22, 1990.
17 St. Josemaría Escrivá, *The Way* (London: Scepter, 1987), no. 495.

Chapter 4

Knowledge Brought to Life: Prayer

The Soul of the Christian Life

I turn again to the importance of harmonizing doctrine and life. The objective knowledge of Christ needs the complement of being lived out. If the truths of the Faith are to change our hearts, they need to be meditated upon in a climate of prayer. As Javier Sesé points out, "[P]rayer is the living expression and the nourishment of this progressive intimacy of love with God of which the Christian spiritual life essentially consists."[1]

The personal encounter with Christ is at once a *gift* that we receive gratuitously and a *task* that nobody can do for us. It entails an interior experience as incommunicable as it is unforgettable, a light that marks our soul and helps us

---

1   Javier Sesé, *Naturaleza y dinamismo de la vida espiritual, Scripta Theologica* 35 (2003): p. 55.

more than reading many books. As one Norwegian convert expresses it,

> Christianity is not a series of moral rules or a philosophical system. It's a relationship with a person. That is its essence. The encounter with Christ may be a sudden shock or a gradual discovery. But it is he who seeks us out in the Mass, or in prayer, in a conversation or in a thought. We want to be loved— this is the deepest desire of our existence—and we find it in the true love of God, through his Son made Man. This is the secret, the hidden love, the pearl of great price."[2]

Without this love relationship with the Lord, Christianity is distorted; it's cheapened and reduced to a mere ideology or ethical system. Religion turned into ideology is always a dangerous thing; it blends in with political opinions, and instead of unifying, it divides. Nor can it be reduced to a series of moral values, as we see with some parents who want a Catholic school for their children, not so much to teach them to love God as to learn rules of behavior. The Christian ideal is something much greater than this: it consists of living for love of the one who, without forcing our free will, does

2   Haaland Matlary, *El amor escondido: La búsqueda del sentido de la vida* (Barcelona: Belacqua, 2002), p. 241.

everything possible to reveal his love for us. Commenting on the conversion of St. Paul, Frossard notes,

> Christianity is not a conception of the world, nor even a rule of life; it is a love story that begins anew with each soul. For the greatest of the apostles, fascinated to the end by the beauty of a face seen on the road to Damascus, the truth is not an idea to be served but a person to be loved.[3]

Love is forged and maintained by dealings with a person. If people who have devoted their lives to God neglect this, they run the risk of falling into *activism*. Instead of working on their apostolic ideal with the aim of pleasing the Lord, their pride brings them to center their attention on the visible results of their efforts. Their decayed "roots" produce ephemeral "fruits." "It looks as though he is using his time well. He seems to get around, to organize things, to be inventing new ways of solving all kinds of problems . . . but he has nothing to show for his efforts."[4] They leave neither trace nor imprint, because their desire for "effectiveness" ends up compromising the *fruitfulness* of the labor. "We have to work a lot on this earth," St. Josemaría counsels:

---

3   André Frossard, *Les grands bergers* (Bilbao, Spain: Desclée de Brouwer, 1992), p.115.

4   Escrivá, *Friends of God*, no. 51.

[W]e must do our work well, since it is our daily tasks that we have to sanctify. But let us never forget to do everything for his sake. If we were to do it for ourselves, out of pride, we would produce nothing but leaves, and no matter how luxuriant they were, neither God nor our fellow men would find any good in them.[5]

Fruits of Prayer

For our mental prayer to be effective, it's usually good to dedicate a fixed time to it each day. There are lots of ways to do this. It's enough to sit down in a church or in some peaceful place and start to chat with the Lord as we would if we could see him. Any subject is fine—he takes an interest in everything that concerns us—although, with the passing of time, our empathy with his heart increases, and we'll be talking less and less of our own concerns and more and more of his. St. Josemaría, in *The Way*, answers someone who wonders what we can talk about with God:

About Him, about yourself: joys, sorrows, successes and failures, noble ambitions, daily worries, weaknesses! And acts of thanksgiving and petitions: and Love and reparation.

5   Escrivá, *Friends of God*, no. 202.

> In a word: to get to know him and to get to
> know yourself: "to get acquainted!"[6]

We can start, perhaps, by commenting on the latest thing that's happened to us, and then go deeper into some spiritual subject. It can be helpful to accompany these times with a book of meditation appropriate to our circumstances, although it's often not necessary, because conversation flows readily. This is the time to ask all kinds of questions. In the depths of our conscience, beyond the manipulable psychological level, we perceive the will of God. Every time we decide to second his inspirations, we experience a profound inner peace. It's like trying to catch a distant frequency on the radio. The Lord, so as to avoid imposing himself, doesn't tend to speak in a very clear way, but little by little we get in tune with him. St. Teresa of Kolkata gives us this advice:

> Never give up this daily intimate contact with Jesus as the real living person—not just the idea. How can we last even one day without hearing Jesus say, "I love you"—impossible. Our soul needs that as much as the body needs to breathe the air. If not, prayer is dead—meditation only thinking. Jesus wants you each to hear him—speaking in the silence of your heart.[7]

6   Escrivá, *The Way*, no. 91.
7   Mother Teresa, "The Fulfillment Jesus Wants for Us," March 25, 1993, Catholic Education Resource Center, https://www.catholiceducation.org/en/religion-and-philosophy/prayer/the-fulfillment-jesus-wants-for-us.html.

With the passing of time, love of the Lord is no longer something known or sensed: it's palpable! We discover that it's not just us seeking him, but that he takes the initiative. "At first it will be more difficult," testifies St. Josemaría.

> You must make an effort to seek out the Lord, to thank him for his fatherly and practical concern for us. Although it is not a question of sentiment, little by little the love of God makes itself felt like a rustle in the soul. It is Christ who pursues us lovingly: "Behold, I stand at the door and knock." How is your life of prayer going? At times don't you feel during the day the impulse to speak more at length with him? Don't you then whisper to him that you will tell him all about it later, in a heart-to-heart conversation?
>
> In the periods expressly reserved for this rendezvous with our Lord, the heart is broadened, the will is strengthened, the mind, helped by grace, fills the world of human reality with supernatural content. The results come in the form of clear, practical resolutions to improve your conduct, to deal more charitably with all men, to spare no efforts— like good athletes—in this Christian struggle of love and peace.[8]

---

8   Escrivá, *Christ Is Passing By*, no. 8.

Indeed, prayer channels and empowers our resolutions to improve. This "hid[den life] with Christ in God" (Col 3:3) changes us on the inside. The wisdom that a Christian who has persevered for years in mental prayer acquires is striking. I was closely acquainted with a man who had never studied but who, with all naturalness, cleared up the doubts that were troubling his interlocutor, a famous professor. He told him, "You just resolved a problem that had me stumped." The simple man saw no problem whatsoever. He had spent almost fifty years praying each day, and he wasn't even aware of how much his master, the Holy Spirit, had taught him.

In essence, we receive light for our *intelligence* and motions of the *will* which bring with them a gradual purification of the *heart*. As we begin to perceive the Lord's love, our will adheres to him and our heart experiences an unsuspected freedom. As long as we try to devote a fixed time to prayer every day, he draws us within his heart. We realize how easy it becomes to love madly someone who has become human like us. We discover not only the *intensity* of his affection, but also the *quality* of his love, which shows itself in abundant deeds of disinterested and detached affection. We realize that he is always looking out for our good and that, far from "keeping accounts," he delicately respects our freedom; he gives himself up for us entirely with a respect that has nothing to do with indifference. In fact, as St. Josemaría says, we begin "to love Jesus, in a more effective way, with the sweet and gentle surprise of his encounter."[9]

Prayer and Charity

In contrast to what those who are wary of a prayer life might believe, claiming that they don't want to neglect love of neighbor, one of the fruits of empathy with Christ's heart consists of intensification of *charity toward others*. "It is not possible," says St. Josemaría, "for our poor nature to be so close to God and not be fired with hunger to sow joy and peace throughout the world."[10] Knowing that the Lord loves each person as himself stimulates our concern to be better parents, brothers, sisters, friends. Knowing the depths of mercy in Jesus and his preaching for those most in need, we learn to be more understanding with the flaws of others, and we make an effort to collaborate in every kind of initiative that seeks to alleviate all kinds of poverty, physical (works of assistance), or spiritual (apostolate).

Those around us always benefit from the progress of our spiritual life. It's something that anyone can see with clarity if they're not bent on reducing Christianity to a philanthropic social ideology. Without the centrality of love of the Person of Christ, the Christian life becomes distorted. It's reduced to a vague ideal, certainly well-intentioned, which tries to

9   Escrivá, *Friends of God*, no. 296.
10   Escrivá, *Friends of God,* no. 311.

bring about a better world—or else a dangerous partisan ideology. To cut charity off from the nutritive soil of the love of the Lord leads necessarily to exhaustion. This is especially evident in those Catholics who are active in public life and systematically neglect their prayer lives. Instead of *Christianizing* the world, they *mundanize* themselves. As the years strip them of their initial activist fervor, uncomfortable moral problems arise, and their integrity is conspicuous only by its absence. It seems that they adhere to the Christian ideal merely for reasons of convenience and abandon it when those motives disappear. The Lord has already told us, "If you love me, you will keep my commandments" (Jn 14:15).

On the other hand, if we don't neglect the interior life, the desire for generous surrender gradually grows. The example of St. Teresa of Kolkata is quite eloquent in this respect. Everything she did to help the poorest of the poor had its roots sunk into her love for Christ. Her spirituality was founded on a mysterious personal encounter she had with him in 1946, while riding a train. She sensed that Jesus was not only thirsty when he was nailed to the Cross (see Jn 19:28), but also thirsted for the love of each one of us now. She understood that she was the only one who could quench the "thirst" that the Lord had for her. She found out, too, that she should alleviate with her love also the "thirst" that our Redeemer feels because of the way he identifies himself with the pain of "the poorest of the poor." That is the deepest answer to why St. Teresa did everything she did throughout her life. In 1993, when she was eighty-three, she had a presentiment that her final days were coming. She wrote a letter in which she summarized her whole experience. Urging her daughters to seek a true encounter with the Lord, she told them,

> Jesus wants me to tell you again, especially in this Holy Week, how much love He has for each one of you—beyond all you can imagine. I worry some of you still have not really met Jesus—one to one—you and Jesus alone. We may spend time in chapel—but have you seen with the eyes of your soul how He looks at you with love? Do you really know the living Jesus—not from books but from being with Him in your heart? Have you heard the loving words He speaks to you? Ask for the grace, He is longing to give it . . . . until you know deep inside that Jesus thirsts for you—you can't begin to know who He wants to be for you. Or who He wants you to be for Him.[11]

11   CLMrf, "'I Thirst'—A Letter from Mother Teresa to Her Sisters," Catholic Life Ministries, April 18, 2019, http://www.catholiclifeministries. org/2019/04/18/4228/.

Treating Christ as a Man

We've already seen that in the Christian life there are spiritualities as diverse as they are legitimate. Another source of variety is the vital context in which each one develops, as well as each one's personal correspondence to grace. Every love story, whether human or divine, is unique and unrepeatable. It's like climbing a mountain, but by different trails to the top. Nonetheless, there are also shortcuts. The teachings of Jesus and the experiences of the saints confirm for us that the best way to dive into divine intimacy comes by way of a trusting relationship with Christ's most holy humanity.

When we speak with Jesus Christ, since the human is more accessible than the divine, it makes sense to distinguish between his two natures. When we're asking him for something, we don't need to go in for a lot of nuances: we address his person in general. On the other hand, if we're drawing near to Jesus really present in the tabernacle to initiate a personal conversation, after dropping to our knees to adore his divinity, it's easier to treat him as a man: we can expound on what's on our mind and pour out all our affection. Besides, as in any love relationship, *affectivity* also plays an important role in these intimate dealings with the Lord. "Since we are carnal and are born of the lust of the flesh," observes St. Bernard, "it must be that our desire and our love shall have its beginning in the flesh."[12] Besides, to love him with all our heart is not just to respond to a need of our own: he also, being human like us, appreciates it. Those who are ignorant of this reality of mutual affection can fall into sentimentalism, that egotistical tendency to enjoy feelings as if they were an end in themselves.

Speaking of Jesus, we can't lose sight of the fact that his feelings haven't changed now that he's in heaven. Reading the Gospel, we perhaps feel a certain envy of his contemporaries—not realizing that we're his contemporaries, too. St. Josemaría, addressing someone who was excited to read the Gospel, told him, "You're contemplating him then as so profoundly human, so much within your reach!" And he adds, "Well . . . Jesus continues being the same as then."[13] Indeed, "Jesus Christ is the same yesterday and today and for ever" (Heb 13:8). In heaven, he continues to feel everything about us and our lives as his own. Paul's vision on the road to Damascus confirms it. Showing his sorrow at the persecution of the Christians, he doesn't say, "Why do you persecute *them*?" but "Why do you persecute *me*?" And when the future apostle asks, "Who are you, Lord?" he replies, "I am Jesus, whom you are persecuting" (Acts 9:4-5). We see that he identifies with each one of the members of his Mystical Body

---

12 St. Bernard of Clairvaux, *On Loving God,* chapter 15. Public Domain.
13 St. Josemaría Escrivá, *Furrow* (New York: Scepter, 1987), no. 233.

on earth. "Christ is now exalted above the heavens," explains St. Augustine, "but he still suffers on earth all the pain that we, the members of his body, have to bear."[14] According to the liturgy, "he ascended not to distance himself from our lowly state, but that we, his members, might be confident of following where he, our Head and Founder, has gone before."[15] For this reason he said that everything we do to one another we do to him (see Mt 25:35–45).

This co-penetration of Christ with each one of us urges us to share, heart to heart, both joys and sorrows. If this harmony of feeling is reciprocal—if we put ourselves in his shoes—the intimate conversation serves not only as an outlet and a comfort to us: he also "benefits." In both directions, the joys intensify and the sadness is lessened. St. Faustina Kowalska recounts that one day Jesus allowed her to contemplate his sorrow due to some sins being committed at that moment. The Lord, seeing her disconsolate, told her, "I see the sincere pain of your heart which brought great solace to My Heart. See and take comfort."[16]

14   St. Augustine, Sermon on the Lord's Ascension, as quoted in Vatican website, https://www.vatican.va/spirit/documents/spirit_20010525_agostino_en.html.

15   Preface I of the Solemnity of the Lord's Ascension.

16   St. Faustina, *Divine Mercy in My Soul: Diary of Saint Maria Faustina Kowalska* (Stockbridge, MA: Marian Fathers of the Immaculate Conception, 1987), no. 445.

During times of prayer, that co-penetration will bring us to *look at Jesus.* Closing our eyes or fixing them on the tabernacle, from which he truly sees us and hears us, we will try to imagine his most loveable and merciful face. It's good for us to remember that nothing in us is unknown to him. It's moving to know that he looks at us with immense affection, even seeing each one of our weak spots. This greatly facilitates our sincerity. Whenever we talk to other people, we tend to hide certain aspects of our inner selves. With him, though, this makes no sense. He only expects us to humbly acknowledge every sin, flaw, and wound, at the same time asking for his forgiveness, so that he can help us and heal us.

After *looking, as Jesus looks at us,* we will attempt to catch a glimpse of his own inner self: we will ask him for light to perceive those joys and sadnesses that his Sacred Heart harbors, and so we will resolve to perform all our actions with the aim of offering him joys. Indeed, looking at the Lord is perhaps the simplest and the deepest way to pray. The famous anecdote of the parishioner who came in each morning to pray at St. John Vianney's church is unforgettable: " I look at him and he looks at me: this is what a certain peasant of Ars in the time of his holy curé used to say while praying before the tabernacle."[17]

---

17   *Catechism,* no. 2715.

Prayer and Contemplation

The itinerary of the spiritual life passes from empathy with Christ to the contemplation of his Triune life. Along the inclined plane of our sanctification the quality of our dealings with the Lord improves gradually. According to St. Josemaría, "The path that leads to holiness is the path of prayer; and prayer ought to take root and grow in the soul little by little, like the tiny seed which later develops into a tree with many branches."[18] We go from less to more. "We start with vocal prayers which many of us have been saying since we were children."[19]

Later, we gain practice in mental prayer until the moment comes when, with a true "prayer of quiet," we ceaselessly contemplate the intimate life of God. Then, besides praising and adoring the holiness of the three divine Persons, we learn to treat them individually, distinguishing each one of them.

Different types of prayer, then, do exist. *Contemplation* is more perfect than *reciting a prayer* or *meditating* on a particular text. Contemplation does not need the effort of the intelligence. If discursive thought had to be present for contemplation, it wouldn't be possible to be contemplatives in the midst of our everyday doings. "One cannot always meditate, but one can always enter into inner prayer,

18   Escrivá, *Friends of God*, no. 295.
19   Escrivá, *Friends of God*, no. 296.

independently of the conditions of health, work, or emotional state."[20] Contemplating consists of *loving while gazing upon* and *gazing while loving* the one who is continually looking at us with love. A person who intuits God's love no longer needs discursive thought. "Words are not needed, because the tongue cannot express itself. The intellect grows calm. One does not reason; one looks! And the soul breaks out once more into song, a new song, because it feels and knows it is under the loving gaze of God, all day long."[21]

Following the example of Opus Dei's founder, it turns out to be possible to live as "contemplatives in the middle of the world."[22] The intimate conversations with the Lord in prayer engrave on the retina of our soul his loving gaze, so that the awareness of being in his presence all day long intensifies. In this way, with a perfect *unity of life*, we learn to materialize the love of God and of others through the vicissitudes of everyday life. We learn, for instance, to do our professional work with the greatest possible perfection for a double motive of charity: to offer it to the Lord as a gift and to serve our neighbor better.

The classic authors distinguish three phases in the spiritual life: the *purgative way*, centered on inner purification; the *illuminative way*, marked by the lights of the Holy Spirit;

20 *Catechism*, no. 2710.
21 Escrivá, *Friends of God*, no. 307.
22 Escrivá, *Christ is Passing By*, no. 174.

and the *unitive way*, which is heaven's antechamber. Although
we can't limit the action of grace in rigid formulas, and
each love story is unrepeatable, that schema can channel
our reflections.

When communicating his gifts, God is less selective than
we might imagine. There are few who reach the highest
summits of contemplative life, and this is due to the lack
of correspondence to grace. A whole *interior purification*
is needed, which requires docility to the motions of the
Holy Spirit, generosity in voluntary sacrifice, and fortitude
in the face of passive purgation. "But do not forget," says
St. Josemaría, "that being with Jesus means we shall most
certainly come upon his Cross."[23] Not many let themselves
be molded without resistance through the trials the Lord
permits. This is how St. John of the Cross explains the
scarcity of contemplatives:

> It should be known that the reason is not that God
> wishes only a few of these spirits to be so elevated;
> he would rather want all to be perfect, but he finds
> few vessels that will endure so lofty and sublime a
> work. Since he tries them in little things and finds
> them so weak that they immediately flee from work,
> unwilling to be subject to the least discomfort and
> mortification, it follows that not finding them strong

23 Escrivá, *Friends of God*, no. 301.

and faithful in that little (Mt. 25:21, 23), in which he favored them by beginning to hew and polish them, he realizes that they will be much less strong in these greater trials. As a result he proceeds no further in purifying them and raising them from the dust of the earth through the toil of mortification. They are in need of greater constancy and fortitude than they showed.[24]

There is much to purify, in the senses as well as in the soul's powers: intellect and will. Ordinarily, the most arduous part is to root out pride. With humble people the Holy Spirit can do marvels because he finds them receptive to all his gifts. The total detachment from our own esteem increases in the soul to the degree that we learn to look at ourselves with the Lord's own merciful eyes. As I tried to show in my last book,[25] this inner transformation floods the soul with peace and accomplishes the most marvelous sense of liberation. And it not only improves our relationship with ourselves, but also with others. The humble self-esteem of knowing how much we're loved purifies and ennobles all our loves.

Apart from that inner purification, progress in the contemplative life requires an *attitude of tireless searching.* The

---

24 St. John of the Cross, *Living Flame of Love*, stanza 2, no. 27.
25 Michel Esparza, *Self Esteem without Selfishness: Increasing Our Capacity for Love* (New York: Scepter, 2013).

Lord is the one who wants our advancement most, but his delicate respect for our freedom leads him to grant his *lights* above all to those who make the greatest effort to know him. As we have already seen, the desire for God, implicit in every human being, becomes more explicit and intense as we intuit the divine goodness. The more we feel God's love, the more we yearn to know him better. St. Josemaría puts it well when he says,

> A thirst for God is born in us, a longing to understand his tears, to see his smile, his face . . . . We have run "like the deer, longing for flowing streams"; thirsting, our lips parched and dry. We want to drink at this source of living water. All day long, without doing anything strange, we move in this abundant, clear spring of fresh waters that leap up to eternal life.[26]

The path that leads to the highest contemplation goes up successive steps. We observe in them a sort of feedback mechanism: every bit of progress makes possible new advances. The more you desire, the more you seek; the more you find, the more you love. St. Anselm condenses this itinerary into this prayer:

> Teach me to seek You, and reveal Yourself to me as I seek; for unless You teach [me] I cannot seek You,

---

26   Escrivá, *Friends of God*, nos. 310 and 307.

and unless You reveal Yourself I cannot find You.
Let me seek You in desiring You; let me desire You
in seeking You. Let me find [You] in loving [You];
let me love [You] in finding [You].[27]

I can't resist copying some eloquent words of St. Josemaría.
They are a whole compendium of the contemplative life,
a masterly expression of the tension of love that a person
experiences who, living in the midst of the world, has arrived
at a high degree of intimacy with the Lord:

First one brief aspiration, then another, and
another . . . till our fervor seems insufficient, because
words are too poor . . . then this gives way to intimacy
with God, looking at God without needing rest or
feeling tired. We begin to live as captives, as prisoners.
And while we carry out as perfectly as we can (with
all our mistakes and limitations) the tasks allotted to us
by our situation and duties, our soul longs to escape. It
is drawn towards God like iron drawn by a magnet.[28]

Persevering in prayer, we also will fall in love with the Lord
to the degree that he grants us his lights. There was a time
when experts in the spiritual life debated the relation between
human efforts (*ascetics*) and divine initiative (*mysticism*).

27   St. Anselm, *Proslogion*, 1, 97–100.
28   Escrivá, *Friends of God*, no. 296.

St. Josemaría settles the question as follows: "Asceticism? Mysticism? I don't mind what you call it. Whichever it is, asceticism or mysticism, does not matter. Either way, it is a gift of God's mercy. If you try to meditate, Our Lord will not deny you his assistance."[29] Indeed, God tends to bless with his lights our efforts to be diligent about keeping to our usual times of prayer, but it's also possible to receive his inspiration without any effort on our own part.

Hellmut Laun, a German convert, received one of those unexpected lights. Suddenly, he understood with great depth the mystery of the *Catholic Church*. He comprehended its greatness by contemplating the glorious open space we will have in heaven once the number of the blessed is complete. He finds no words to describe it, but he attempts to:

> Everything I had read about the Catholic Church, one and holy, before my conversion, was completely true . . . but it was hardly a shadow compared to the blinding supernatural beauty of the Church triumphant! Not even a thousand words carefully selected could ever describe the vision that we will have of the Church of Christ in its final and full reality, in one single glance, in the other life, when we are contemplating God's goodness and wisdom. What innumerable saints have said of the

29   Escrivá, *Friends of God*, no. 308.

Church is without a doubt true. An inexpressibly
glorious reality![30]

The lights that help us most to progress on the road to union
with God are linked to the indwelling of the Most Holy
Trinity in our soul. Ordinarily, meditating on the Trinitarian
mystery, we are grateful to God that his greatness doesn't
fit in our own little heads, but sometimes we are filled with
joy upon receiving some flash of illumination. "Our heart,"
testifies St. Josemaría,

> now needs to distinguish and adore each one of the
> divine Persons. The soul is, as it were, making a
> discovery in the supernatural life, like a little child
> opening his eyes to the world about him. The soul
> spends time lovingly with the Father and the Son
> and the Holy Spirit, and readily submits to the work
> of the life-giving Paraclete, who gives himself to us
> with no merit on our part, bestowing his gifts and
> the supernatural virtues![31]

Since we are called to participate in that divine life, let's go
deeper into the contemplation of *heavenly beatitude*. In heaven,
thanks to the *beatific vision*, we will live fully the same thing
which, though in a veiled way, is already happening in our

---

30   Hellmut Laun, *Cómo Encontré a Dios* [How I met God] (Madrid: Ediciones
      Rialp, 1986), p. 163.
31   Escrivá, *Friends of God*, no. 306.

soul in grace inhabited by the Trinity: the Father is loving us in the Holy Spirit like sons in the Son.

Contemplation and Imagining Heaven

Imagining heaven is a great incentive for our hope. We live, as the liturgy says, "in hope of the glorious coming of our Lord Jesus Christ." We are on a journey, and it makes sense that our thoughts should escape to our final destination, waiting for the Person who loves us most and best. If we love him madly, we ardently desire definitive union with him.

Let's try to give ourselves an idea of heaven, since we can't desire what we haven't imagined. For this task, those authors who describe it as something tedious and unattractive are of no help. Louis de Wohl, an expert in war intelligence, comments scornfully,

> The fellow who invented the stuff about the little clouds, the harp music, and the incessant singing was without doubt very inspired. But not about heaven. It's one of the most dangerous works of infernal propaganda. Since it's not possible to describe heaven as *bad*, they describe it as extremely boring. And the Satanic Ministry of Propaganda collaborates here with a fault in our human nature. We have a much greater facility for imagining hell than heaven . . . . Is it possible that evil is more familiar to us than is good? That would be quite an alarming thought.

> How many idiotic jokes has this deformed image
> of heaven given rise to! We hear all the time that
> hell must be much more fun than heaven, because
> surely that's where all the interesting people are; in
> heaven, on the other hand, are only the honorable
> people, the exemplary boys and girls, nauseatingly
> boring, singing in chorus and playing the harp.[32]

Beatitude doesn't come only from contemplating God. It also offers human elements. In Christ, God was made man without detriment to his divinity. So, too, we will be divinized without being dehumanized. Our risen bodies will acquire a spiritualized but not a dematerialized state. Thus, every noble human reality will have its corollary in heaven. There we will live a family life with the rest of the blessed. Besides loving God, we will also love each of them more and better than we were ever able to love them on earth. Consequentially, as Thomas Aquinas recalls, each other's happiness will become our own.[33] To imagine it, we'd have to multiply that joy by the enormous number of the blessed.

Let's leave aside those "human" aspects of heaven and focus on our participation in God's own intimate life. St. Paul's testimony is eloquent: "What no eye has seen, nor

---

32 Louis De Wohl, *Adam, Eve and the Ape*, (Chicago: Henry Regnery, 1960).
33 See St. Thomas Aquinas, collation regarding *Credo in Deum*, art. 12, in *Summa Theologica* 2.

ear heard, nor the heart of man conceived, what God has prepared for those who love him" (1 Cor 2:9).[34] What will the joy that comes of knowing and loving God the way he knows and loves us be like (see 1 Cor 13:12, 1 Jn 3:2)? We already know that the divine is not altogether imaginable by virtue of its analogy with the human. Practically, human love of a high caliber is the best source of inspiration.

The key to happiness, in human love as in divine, resides above all in the quality of the intentions of those who love. Only God's love, which lacks nothing, is entirely *gratuitous*. St. Bernard describes that unequaled perfection in these terms: "Love is sufficient of itself, it gives pleasure by itself and because of itself. It is its own merit, its own reward. Love looks for no cause outside itself, no effect beyond itself. Its profit lies in its practice. I love because I love, I love that I may love."[35] We ourselves don't rise to such a level: what we aspire to is *rectitude of intention*. What is this? Our inner life is complex. One and the same action can be inspired by various motives. These are right to the degree that they don't place a person's own advantage above the good of the beloved person. The person who gives in order to receive something

---

34   See also Is 64:4.

35   St. Bernard of Clairvaux, *On the Canticle of Canticles*, no. 83, 4, as quoted in "St. Bernard of Clairvaux," Crossroads Initiative, August 16, 2021, https://www.crossroadsinitiative.com/media/articles/love-of-bridegroom-and-bride-st-bernard-of-clairvaux/.

in return is not disinterested. *To love* is the opposite of *to use*. It is the will to *belong*, not to *possess*. Due to our limitations, our motivation is never entirely altruistic. We may harbor *sincere intentions* if we avoid all conscious deception. The degree of disinterestedness in our actions increases to the extent that we are perfected. Grace and good will progressively mitigate that egotism and self-love that cloud our intentions.

Two persons joined in a highly disinterested love experience a happiness that's difficult to describe. Their reciprocal devotion produces a surprising *spiral of happiness* that plunges them into an unhoped-for bliss, which allows them a foretaste of divine beatitude. To the extent that they're not pursuing their own advantage, the happiness they procure, so to speak, "bounces off them" at least twice. In an ideal marriage, if the husband brings his wife a gift, her happiness comes back to him. In its turn, this sweet surprise reverberates in her. And it all remains. If we throw a pebble into the water, it produces a certain number of concentric circles. If there were no friction, the circles would continue spreading, as with an object being pushed beyond the pull of gravity.

Something of the same sort must happen among the divine Persons because of the infinite purity of their love, although, by virtue of their eternal perfection, we must rule out any kind of succession or change. For the blessed, on the other hand, as some theologians posit, comes a crescendo of blessedness: participating in this fullness of divine joy, they experience an enduring spiral of beatitude. We can't visualize the result of multiplying infinitely the greatest joy we've ever felt in this life, but we know at least which amount would be infinitely multiplied.

And that isn't all! When we're imagining inconceivable celestial beatitude, at the *maximum purity* of divine love, we can add six new elements:

1. *Infinite wisdom* (we will know everything down to the last why)
2. *Full reciprocity*
3. *Eternal duration*
4. *Complete understanding* (total absence of misunderstandings and mistrust)
5. *Total absence of worry* about the future of the love relationship (the impossibility of competition or betrayal)
6. Infinite perfection and *beauty of the beloved person*

Speaking of that divine loveliness, St. Josemaría states,

> Consider what is most beautiful and most noble on earth, what pleases the mind and the other faculties, and what delights the flesh and the senses.
>
> And the world, and the other worlds that shine in the night: the whole universe. Well this, along with

all the follies of the heart satisfied, is worth nothing, is nothing and less than nothing compared . . . with this God of mine!—of yours! Infinite treasure, pearl of great price.[36]

Considering all these aspects, an ineffable joy can be glimpsed. What will it be like to be immersed in this *looking at each other and loving, and loving each other and looking*, between God and each one of the blessed? According to St. John of the Cross, God says to the soul, "I am yours, and for you, and I love to be as I am to be yours and to give myself to you."[37] If we remember that we are already, now, being loved as we will be in heaven, it will be easier to live as contemplatives in the middle of the world.

Once every resource of reason is exhausted, if we intuit the inexpressible, "we must make room for the 'chaste silence' that Pseudo-Dionysius spoke of regarding the names of God."[38] Because, when speaking of love, a time comes when it is better to keep silent and experience it! And the more we live it, the more the desire to consummate our union with God in heaven once and for all increases. If we sense what awaits us there, we possess a sort of frozen image which, upon our entry into eternity, will be set in motion. In the

36   Escrivá, *The Way*, no. 432.

37   St. John of the Cross, *Living Flame of Love*, stanza 3, no. 6.

38   Carlos Cardona, *Metafísica del bien y del mal* (Pamplona: EUNSA, 1988), p. 131.

meantime, let us purify our longings, remembering that God, being the one who loves most, is the one who most desires that eternal union.

From Mary, who was accustomed to ponder all things in her heart, let us learn to be contemplatives in the midst of our everyday affairs. If, with the help of grace, we are faithful down to the end of our life, the veils that hide the Lord will tear and we will finally see him face to face. The unknown always entails something disquieting. But when we reach heaven, we will immediately feel at home, since our mother will come out to receive us.

Part 2

CO-REDEEMING
WITH CHRIST

Chapter 5

A Debt of Gratitude

Why Complicate Our Life?

The point of encounter between our own intimacy and the Lord's, uniquely enriched through prayer, leads spontaneously to a series of fruits and practical consequences. Empathy with the heart of Jesus urges us on to action, to sacrifice—in short, to "complicate" our existence, in the most positive sense of the word, when it comes to loving God and other people. Baptism, by transforming us into "other Christs" (see Gal 2:19–20),[1] makes us able to participate actively in his work of Redemption. Our life thus takes on a deep sense of mission, which leads us to seek out all kinds of opportunities to show our love with deeds and help him to save souls.

It's a fact, however, that the Lord, so often, doesn't figure among the motives that move a Christian's life. He seems

---

1   See also Rom 6:4 and Phil 2:5.

like the great forgotten. Many people with faith invoke all kinds of reasons, most of them of a personal nature, to defend their religious practice, but very seldom do they shine the spotlight on love, which is the main motor for "complicating" a person's life. They touch upon matters such as how their life of piety helps them not to neglect it as in past years, that it helps them to be happier, to conquer egotism more easily—thus, treating other people better—and, as a last resort, to ensure their eternal salvation. But they forget the whole other dimension: to be aware that it is Christ himself who urges on our love the most, to alleviate the sadness of his heart.

"Training" in the Christian life is carried out on an inclined plane. Early on, egocentric motives usually predominate. As we mature, we come to see that nothing matters as much as our relations of love with the Lord. In the catechesis of Christian initiation, we ought to imitate the pedagogy employed by God with revelation: to teach first the basic truths of the Old Testament and then complete them with that full truth of the gospel which is rooted in love.

As empathy with Christ increases, at some point everything we do seems too little. The intensity with which the saints live their lives is the best way of illustrating this change. They leave no sacrifice undone that might offer the Lord any joy and help him to save souls. The examples are innumerable. Let's recall St. Teresa of Ávila, grappling with all sorts of obstacles, founding convents amid the discomforts of sixteenth-century transportation. Or St. Anthony Mary Claret, who at age sixty-three had preached ten thousand sermons and published more than two hundred books. In just the seven years that he was a bishop in Cuba, he administered the Sacrament of Confirmation to three hundred thousand people and arranged thirty thousand marriages. Without a doubt, God bestowed on these saints some exceptional human talents, but this is not enough to explain their indefatigable activity. Their apostolic zeal has its roots in their love for the Lord. Like St. Paul, they felt that above all, the love of Christ urged them on (see 2 Cor 5:14).

For us to decide to "complicate" our lives more for the same reasons as the saints, we need to love the Lord madly. Broadly speaking, two paths lead us to love a person greatly: *gratitude* at the experience of their goodness, and *compassion* upon seeing them suffer. The head understands gratitude, while the heart sympathizes easily with the sorrows of others; the intelligence presses on to seek ways to remedy those sorrows and urges the will to put them into practice. Our response to Christ's love at first moves us above all to see that nobody deserves our devotion more: "love is repaid by love" (*amor con amor se paga*). As time passes and our affections are more and more in tune with his most holy humanity, we burn inwardly with a pressing urgency to alleviate the sorrows of his heart.

So we have at our disposal two driving forces to spur our generosity. Which of the two is more powerful: gratitude to Jesus for the greatness of his love for us, or compassion for his Sacred Heart? In practice, we can see that gratitude isn't usually a sufficient motivation for loving God with such madness. To repay him for his love, perhaps we'll be disposed to pray frequently, to come punctually to the sacraments, or to be diligent about our religious formation. This is a lot, but it's not sufficient.

The saints go much further: even when they're working their fingers to the bone, everything still seems too little to them. Why? Clearly, not because they're perfectionists, and not solely out of gratitude. What motivates their heroic effort is their empathy for the sorrowful heart of Christ and the consequent urgency of alleviating that pain. The certainty of being able to lessen his redemptive sufferings spurs their generosity more powerfully. The motives of compassion that the wounds of his heart inspire turn out to be more imperious than those born of mere gratitude.

This, then, is our road map: first, we will consider the reasons for gratitude for the Lord's love for each one of us, and then, we will go deeper into the urgency of co-redeeming with Christ.

Being Grateful for Love

Love is the *gratuitous* gift *par excellence.* A person may be grateful for any gift, but nothing is so fitting as to give *thanks* for the love received. Thus, pondering all the different paths by which God manifests his love to us gives rise to a gratitude that urges us to respond to that love. Prayer helps us to sense how much the Lord has done and continues to do for each of us. We realize, for example, how his loving providence has diligently arranged all the circumstances of our life so that they work together for what is best. Or we're struck when we consider the madness of the love entailed in the Incarnation, seeing God himself "humbled, become a slave, reduced to the form of a servant in the stable where he chose to be born, in Joseph's workshop, in his Passion and in his ignominious death . . . and in the madness of Love which is the blessed Eucharist."[2] If we *feel* that love, a moment will come in which everything we do for the Lord will seem like nothing. And then those early egocentric motives will no longer be what move us most. Then we will want above all to meet love with love. How well that anonymous sixteenth-century sonnet expresses it:

> The heaven you have promised me, my God,
> Does not move me to love you,
> Nor does hell, so feared,

2   Escrivá, *The Way*, no. 432.

Move me to cease to offend you because of this.
You it is who move me, Lord!
Moved to see you nailed to the cross and derided,
To see your body so wounded;
Your indignities and your death.
What moves me, in the end, is your love, and in
    such a way
That if there were no heaven, still I would love you.
If there were no hell, still I would fear you.
You need not give me anything for my love for you,
For even if I did not hope for as much as I hope for,
I would love you as much as I love you.

Let us meditate on the mercies we've received from God, one by one. Apart from the talents he has given us—such as a particular vocation or a certain aptitude—the Lord has created and redeemed all of us equally. We could compile a whole catalog of the gifts derived from those two realities: from him we receive life, an immortal soul, our intelligence and freedom, revelation and the Faith, and the Church. The list of the gifts of grace would be interminable: the effusion of the Holy Spirit and his indwelling in our soul; divine filiation and the prospect of eternal salvation; the sacraments; the forgiveness of our sins and the healing of our egotism; his silent but Real Presence in every tabernacle; the chance to be present for and participate in the work of Redemption every time we attend Holy Mass; Eucharistic Communion; the mercy and human affection of his Sacred Heart. The final gift given to us by Jesus, on the Cross, is his mother.

Being Grateful for the Church and for Mary

Out of this long list of gifts, it's worth underlining the immense one which is the *Church*, all the more now that it is suffering so many attacks. It's a family that is at once divine and human. It's divine in that its members are intimately joined with a supernatural bond, and it's human in that it prolongs the most marvelous home that has ever existed: that of Jesus, Mary, and Joseph in Nazareth.

We believe in the Church for the same reason that we adhere to the other truths infallibly revealed by the Son of God. We have all the more reason to be grateful for the existence of this family because, through it, Christ guarantees us assurance in doctrine (see Mt 16:18–19).[3] To the Holy Father, his vicar on earth, he promises not infallibility of *conduct* but of *doctrine*. Of the three ministries entrusted to the Church—to teach, to sanctify, and to reign—Jesus Christ ensured the effectiveness of the first two: there is no error possible in dogma, and the effectiveness of validly administered sacraments is assured. On the other hand, when

---

3 On this delegated power, see also Lk 22:31–32; Jn 21:15–17; 1 Cor 4:2.

it comes to ordering the life of the Church, there is always room for improvement.

To appreciate the great gift of the Church, we have to transcend what is visible and focus on what is essential. For example, when we receive a sacrament, little does it matter how imperfect is the priest who administers it, because we know that Jesus Christ himself confers it. Likewise, since the Church is the Mystical Body of Christ, we don't doubt her holiness in the face of the patent wretchedness of some Catholics, since we remember that its *Head* is Jesus Christ, its *soul* the Holy Spirit, and that most of its members are saints already in heaven. Still, we are pained by our own sins and those of others, all the more if we are in sync with the sorrow they cause the heart of Jesus, but that does not dampen our affection toward the one we love like a mother.

"The Church," says St. Josemaría,

> which is divine, is also human . . . for it is made up of men, and men have their defects . . . . When the Lord permits human weakness to appear, our reaction ought to be the same as if we were to see our mother ill or treated with disdain: to love her all the more, to bestow on her a greater manifestation of affection, both external and internal.[4]

---

4   St. Josemaría Escrivá, *Loyalty to the Church,* in *In Love with the Church* (New York: Scepter, 2007), nos. 6 and 7.

The idealistic are excessively shocked by others' weaknesses as if all of us on earth were perfect. Jesus Christ, on the other hand, is very realistic. Precisely because he knows us so well, he preaches of perfection as well as mercy, and he expects of us a holiness that is not incompatible with an acknowledged weakness that is struggled against. Therefore, he chose St. Peter as the first pope, thus founding "the Church on cowardice and repentance."[5] Being unaware of the reality of human failure "will always be the temptation of pride, seemingly angelic and radically demonic. Christ left us his cry of perfection, and that delightful structure of restraints, pardons, and remedies for imperfection which is the Church."[6]

The Church, the effectiveness of the sacraments, and the motherhood of Mary are mysteries intimately related to one another because they all have their origin in Golgotha. These are all graces that flow from Christ's open side on the Cross. Both the Eucharist and Mary *make* us into a family. The members of this human and supernatural family which is the Church take nourishment from the same bread and sit around the same table; we are brothers and sisters of Jesus by being at the same time children of God and of Mary. For this reason, St. Paul writes that God the Father has predestined us

---

5   Pemán, *La Pasión según Pemán* (Madrid: Edibesa, 1997), p. 73.

6   Pemán, p. 74.

"to be conformed to the image of his Son, in order that he might be the first-born among many brethren" (Rom 8:29).

On the Cross, Jesus begged his mother to receive us as her children (see Jn 19:27). Upon accepting, Mary became the *Mother of the Church*. It was no little thing that he was asking of her. He wanted her to accompany us with her motherly care all the way along our path to heaven. And not only those who are alive now, but all those who would be on earth until the end of time. By the will of Jesus, and thanks also to Mary's loving consent, we are, then, children of the most gracious of mothers. From then on, we have to be grateful for such vigilance of a good mother. How much we need her! We are like children who live without a worry in the world as long as they're near their mother.

Gratitude excites devotion. Before he died, Jesus didn't just ask Mary to receive us as children. In the person of John, he also wanted us to welcome her as a mother. This entails caring for her diligently, showing her our affection every day with compliments and deeds. This advice from St. Josemaría is a good summary of the Christian life: "Don't just go to the Virgin Mary to ask her for things. You should also go to give!: give her your affection; give her your love for her divine Son; and show her your affection with deeds of service to others, who are also her children."[7]

---

7   St. Josemaría Escrivá, *The Forge* (New York: Scepter, 1987), no. 137.

CHAPTER 6

CREATION, SIN, AND REDEMPTION

That "Inconvenient" Responsible Freedom

Before we explore co-redemption with Christ, it will be a good idea to investigate the origin of the problem he came to remedy, situating his work of Redemption within the framework of God the Father's creative design. When we ask why there's so much evil in the world, and why Jesus died on the Cross, we confront the reality of sin and freedom. If we don't accept the consequences derived from the misuse of freedom, sin ceases to make any sense, and so does the Redemption. People who don't accept their own responsibility don't even pose the most crucial questions of existence: Who can save me? How do I obtain forgiveness for my sins? What must I do to make sure divine mercy, not justice, has the last word?

The first obstacle that the "new evangelization" confronts
in the West is that most of its targets don't have any sense that
they need to be redeemed and saved. They are not aware, for
various reasons, that they need to be cured of their egotism
and that their eternity is at stake and depends on how they use
they use their freedom in this life. Sometimes what weighs
most heavily in this attitude is the lack of religious formation;
in other cases, a certain anesthesia in the soul blinds them
to what lies beyond the mere sensory, or to not see beyond
everyday concerns that are both unavoidable and ephemeral.

Under such circumstances, speaking of the eternal
promises of Christ is like trying to sell a product to people
who don't think they need it. And if we attempt to pull
them out of their agnostic indifference by speaking to them
about heaven, they'll usually answer, "Yes, it exists, and no
doubt I deserve to go there; I don't do anybody any harm."
They don't stop to think that *evil* is, above all, the privation
of *good*. If he lived in our day, St. Paul would tell them, "Do
not be deceived; God is not mocked, for whatever a man
sows, that he will also reap" (Gal 6:7). It is certainly a pity
that they do not realize the temporal and eternal happiness
that they are missing out on.[1] What can we do in this case?

---

1   St. Josemaría observes that truth is inseparable from joy: "[H]appiness in
     heaven is for those who know how to be happy on earth." Escrivá, *Forge*,
     no. 1005.

First, it's good to show that our decisions do have consequences. Any effort to foster dialogue between reason and faith should begin with underlining that we are ethical beings and therefore free. These days, there's abundant talk of *freedom* and very little of *responsibility*. To avoid dealing with the consequences of their actions, many shield themselves behind a sort of *natural do-goodism* which blames not the person but genetic, educational, or social shortcomings; some even dare to blame God for the evil in the world.

One concrete means of counteracting that *culture of irresponsibility* consists of shining a spotlight on its contradictions and incoherence. We frequently see, for instance, that people who hide behind determinism to avoid their own responsibility change their opinions radically when they're the ones being harmed; in that case, they don't hesitate to insist on the full weight of the law falling upon the guilty party. Whether we realize it or not, deep inside we all know that we're responsible to the extent that we're free. Thus it is that, when judging some reprehensible action, we wonder whether the culprit *truly had a choice*.

Realism, then, leads us to see freedom as the prime mover in our actions, without forgetting that despite the conditions, it's ordinarily the person himself who finally decides. Nobody doubts, for instance, the great influence of education, but it would be absurd to think that this blots out the role of free will when it comes to action. In the end, without free will, we would be like animals: our behavior would always be predictable. But it is not. On the contrary, as a survivor of Auschwitz explains, even under the most extreme conditions, one "may rise above himself, may grow beyond himself, and by so doing change himself."[2]

Acknowledging the existence of responsible freedom allows us to recognize other realities that are equally undeniable: merit and blame, justice, judgment, recompense, and punishment. Strictly speaking, every good or evil deed has its consequences. In their turn, those natural truths facilitate our understanding of Christian doctrine, which teaches that "we must all appear before the judgment seat of Christ, so that each one may receive good or evil, according to what he has done in the body" (2 Cor 5:10). Only God knows the exact degree of freedom involved in each human act. Therefore, it's good that he and he alone should be our judge.

If we all know that we're free, how can anyone deny the obvious? This denial, on many occasions, masks an eagerness to justify a person's own weakness or lack of integrity: some have ceased to live by what they believed because it became more comfortable to believe according to how they lived. Little by little, this *self-deception* leads us away from the truth.

---

2   Victor Frankl, *Man's Search for Meaning* (Boston: Beacon Press, 2006), p. 146.

The failure to recognize our own mistakes—something that requires a good dose of humility and honesty—has become acute in recent years through ignorance of God's love. It is also, therefore, a lack of formation: if we don't know how delighted God is to forgive our sins, there are only two alternatives: acknowledge them and fall into dejection, or deceive ourselves.

The path of *isolated self-deception* is also widespread on the social level, leading to a kind of *collective obliviousness*. *Life* influences *ideas*, and these, in turn, shape *culture* and are reflected in *laws*. The darkening of the conscience affects the most vulnerable points of our moral conduct, such as sexuality, and winds up corrupting essential ethical values. Think, for example, of legal permissiveness with regard to abortion, which is similar to the tolerance that existed in some countries up until the nineteenth century for the slave trade. Such blights only disappear when the *distortion of reason* that self-deception entails comes to an end.[3]

Sadly, we can see in many Christians how this cultural atmosphere fosters irresponsibility. It's discouraging to observe that they don't often stop to think of the ultimate consequences of their decisions, more preoccupied with selecting the right life insurance than with grasping the

---

3   As Benedict XVI affirmed in the British Parliament, "Such misuse of reason, after all, was what gave rise to the slave trade." Address at Westminster Hall (September 17, 2010). Vatican website: www.vatican.va.

eternal realities. Even many priests avoid alluding clearly to
these matters. At funerals, for example, they tend to highlight,
in a stereotypical way, the hope in the Resurrection, but
they omit the calls to conversion that are so abundant in the
Gospel (see Mt 7:21).[4] Those who only come to church on
such occasions might get the idea that salvation is automatic.
It's urgent, therefore, to announce the whole truth, even if it
hurts. Authentic charity demands doing so in an affable but
clear manner. The truth is, "we Christians should be hard
of head and tender of heart."[5]

Knowing the truth beforehand makes us realistic. Those
who don't face up to the eternal implications of their acts must
be made to see two things: that you have to ask forgiveness
of sins so that God's *mercy* can have the last word, and that,
even so, *justice* always has something to say, because, as St. Paul
notes, "he who sows sparingly will also reap sparingly, and
he who sows bountifully will also reap bountifully" (2 Cor
9:6). In accordance with God's mercy, if someone confesses
at the last moment of his life, all his sins will be forgiven,
but he needs to do penance in purgatory to understand,
among other things, how to repent purely for love of God.
Afterwards, given that it's just for the way he lived on earth
to shape his eternity, he will receive a heaven to the measure

4   See also Mt 24:42–51.
5   Jacques Maritain in Vittorio Messori and Andrea Tornielli, Por qué creo:
     Una vida para dar razón de la fe (Madrid: Libros libres, 2009), p. 354.

of his merits. Thus the importance of taking advantage of the time we have.

The saints teach that what should spur our generosity most of all is *compassion* for the heart of Jesus—without neglecting a *sense of responsibility.* "I have to render an account to God for what I've done," St. Josemaría used to say, "and I ardently wish to save my soul."[6] Blotting out the logic of justice is a sign of ignorance or recklessness: we don't need to be afraid of God but of ourselves. The parable of the talents (see Mt 25:14–30) is a disquieting and consoling one: we will receive according to how much we have been given, and what is asked of us is according to our abilities, neither more nor less. At any rate, let's not only be mindful of the harm that sin causes us. Let's consider, too, that it hurts the Lord in accordance with the greatness of his love for us. If we love him, we won't lose sight of this other side of the coin.

The Plan for Creation and the Sorrow of God

Every moral decision we make throughout our lives brings us closer to or farther from the greatest happiness. In practice, sin always damages the one who commits it: lovelessness "alienates man from God, and alienates man from himself

6   Andrés Vázquez de Prada, *The Founder of Opus Dei*, vol. 2 (New York: Scepter, 2003), pp. 294, 420–426.

and from others."[7] The sinner, then, is not the only one to suffer. Those who love him most are also harmed, as well as the possible victims of that moral disorder. The consequences are not trivial. Leaving aside the sum of all the everyday sufferings that don't make it into the papers, we shudder to think, for example, of the millions of people who died in the twentieth century under the Nazi extermination or the Communist terror. In Ukraine alone, to cite a little-known example, Stalin let seven million innocents die of hunger in the winter of 1932–1933, on top of another eleven million who were executed in only four years, between 1937 and 1941. More recent examples include the two million Cambodians (twenty percent of the population) massacred between 1975 and 1979 under the dictatorship of the Khmer Rouge.

These horrifying figures invite us to reflect on the ultimate origin of so much misery, or to ask why God created a world in which such atrocities could occur. Without creation, evil would not exist; for this reason, it's said that God "made" it. Still, on balance, it must be worth it, since without creation, goodness could not have existed either. It would be unjust if, by the fault of those who use their freedom wrongly, many more would not have received

7   St. John Paul II, Apostolic Letter on Keeping the Lord's Day Holy *Dies Domini* (May 31, 1998), no. 63.

the gifts of life and eternal salvation. In any case, blaming God while eluding our own responsibility reveals a smug and disrespectful attitude toward the Creator, as well as ingratitude and injustice, since he is the one who suffers most from the harm our sins bring with them. But admitting that creation was worth the trouble doesn't delegitimize the attempt to understand why.

We will never comprehend, in all its depth, the mystery of evil.[8] Still, we know that love is the only reason God drew us out of nothingness. In an act at once creative and loving, God chose to give us being so that we could participate in his beatitude. But that happiness, being tied to love, requires a freedom which, like a double-edged sword, opens itself up to the best and worst uses. Thus, evil appears. God does not will it. He tolerates it so that beings capable of being transformed into sons and daughters could exist—beings who could freely receive all their father's love. This is what's primordial. The visible universe is accidental: sheer embellishment for the

---

8 We're concerned above all with the origin of *moral evil*, which arises from the evil use of freedom on the part of human beings and fallen angels (demons), which introduced, and continues to introduce, suffering into the world. Let us leave aside *ontological evil*: that limitation of the creature in comparison with God, which is inherent in the fact of creating. God could have made us more perfect, like the angels, but they too have free will, and when they abused their freedom it gave rise to a greater pain and suffering. Nor will we be concerned with *physical evil*, that deterioration of the material world mysteriously introduced by original sin, which brought with it disease and natural disasters.

world we inhabit. By creating it with such largesse, he reveals to us his infinite omnipotence and makes it easy for us to praise him. But for him, one of us is worth more than the whole rest of the universe. We are the "only creature that God has willed for itself."[9]

God decided to create us, fully accepting the risk of our freedom, even though he was aware that there would be no going back and that, if we went astray, he would be the primary victim of the gift he was bestowing. "In a certain sense," St. John Paul II contends, "we might say that *in the face of human freedom God has wished to make himself 'impotent'* . . . . He remains coherent before such a gift."[10] Hence, "the mysterious greatness of personal freedom consists of the way God himself halts before it and respects it."[11]

Our freedom is truly something overpowering. Benedict XVI even speaks of "our inverse omnipotence," since "God cannot enter my heart unless I open the door to him."[12] The point is, God doesn't oblige us to love him, because he loves with such finesse. He waits on our response, because he knows that love is something that persons can only *demand*

9   St. Paul VI, *Gaudium et Spes*, no. 24.
10   St. John Paul II, *Crossing the Threshold of Hope* (New York: Knopf, 1994), pp. 64–65.
11   Edith Stein (St. Teresa Benedicta of the Cross), *Pensamientos* [Thoughts] (Madrid: Monte Carmelo, 1999), p. 50.
12   Benedict XVI, Urbi et Orbi Message (December 25, 2012). Vatican website: www.vatican.va.

of themselves. We can *attract* another's love but not claim it. Failing to adapt to this most basic of rules is one of the most frequent mistakes people make in family life: "to expect the spouse or children to change 'because I said so' is as presumptuous as it is absolutely futile."[13]

At any rate, *divine filiation* is the essential reason for creation. The analogy with human fatherhood allows us to intuit the divine design. However many children good parents have, each one can count on all their affection as if he or she were an only child. And if a child goes astray, they will spare no effort to help them. Likewise, God cares for each of us in particular: you could say he only knows how to have "only children." It is one and the same fatherly love that led him to create us and, after our wrong turn, to find every possible means of saving us (Incarnation and Redemption). He didn't create us assembly-line-style but gave us each, one by one, an immortal soul. Even if people are conceived by egotistical parents, it can't be denied that they're on earth because somebody loved them.

God is, in summary, a Father who loves each of his children as much as he loves himself. As a result, he "begs the love of his creature: He is thirsty for the love of every one of us."[14] In some sense, then, he exposes himself to

13 Ugo Borghello, *Las crisis del amor* (Madrid: Ediciones Rialp, 2003), p. 167.
14 Benedict XVI, Message for Lent 2007 (November 21, 2006). Vatican website: www.vatican.va.

suffering, because to love "is to commit oneself, to make oneself vulnerable and indigent in hopes of some response to this devotion."[15] When we allude to "God's suffering," many assume that we're speaking figuratively. At first, something tells them that an infinitely perfect Being cannot suffer. And they are correct, because God is infinitely happy. Moreover, he is *impassible* (not susceptible to suffering), for which reason they assert that "suffering" can't mean "passively undergoing suffering" as we do, because we experience passions. It is also true, however, that God loves man infinitely so that, as Sacred Scripture confirms (see Hos 11:8–9),[16] he cannot remain indifferent to our sins and sorrows. That means that our offenses and sufferings have to *affect him* in some way, though a way compatible with the infinite perfection of his divine being.

Divine *sorrow*, then, is ineffable but real. It's not easy to find the right wording for this unfathomable mystery. In any case, it's up to the theologians to describe it in the most precise language, although we can also employ anthropomorphic or poetic language; less precise, but still, in a certain way, close to the truth, as when we claim, for instance, that sin "hurts" God like a thorn nailed into his heart. Let's pause briefly before this great mystery, learning from the highly

15   Guillermo Magro, *Los caminos de Dios en la tierra, Scripta Theologica* 31 (1999): p. 521.

16   See also Mt 25:34–35; 28:20; Lk 15:11–32; Acts 9:4; 22:7–8.

reverent attitude with which the most recent popes, and certain other authors we'll be citing, have approached this delicate question.

The *Catechism of the Catholic Church* recalls this phrase from St. Augustine: God "thirsts that we may thirst for him."[17] St. John Paul II, wondering how sin affects the inscrutable divine inner life, affirms cautiously: "The concept of God as the necessarily most perfect being certainly excludes from God any pain deriving from deficiencies or wounds; but in the 'depths of God' there is a Father's love that, faced with man's sin, in the language of the Bible reacts so deeply as to say: I am sorry that I have made him."[18] We might say, ultimately, that nothing and no one can *bind* God except his love. Therefore, in a mysterious but real sense, that love brings with it a "poverty": one that implies no imperfection whatsoever.[19] In fact, God's being essentially *impassible* does not mean he is *indifferent*. As Benedict XVI recalls, "The

---

17 *Catechism*, no. 2560; see St. Augustine, Question 64, 4.

18 St. John Paul II, Encyclical on the Holy Spirit in the Life of the Church and the World Dominum et Vivificantem (May 18, 1986), no. 39. Vatican website: www.vatican.va. The biblical citation is from Gn 6:7.

19 Carlos Cardona, *Metafísica del bien y del mal* (Pamplona: EUNSA, 1987), p. 125, explains it as follows: given that God "loves me, he has intentionally identified himself with me, I am his 'alter ego' now, and my evil becomes his in me, in such a way that it could truly be said that my sin 'hurts God. Whoever doesn't understand this lacks understanding of love, knows nothing of that transference that love brings about. Whoever thinks that our sins don't 'affect' the divine immutability neglects this 'elective mutability,' the vulnerability that love entails. God, by loving me, has become vulnerable in me."

Christian faith has taught us that . . . . God—Truth and Love personified—desired to suffer for us and with us. St. Bernard of Clairvaux coined the marvellous expression: *Impassibilis est Deus, sed non incompassibilis*—God cannot suffer, but he can *suffer with*."[20]

It is altogether possible that all this reasoning is of no great help when it comes to handling the idea of God's *sorrow*, but that doesn't matter if we establish a clear distinction between its *theoretical* explication and its *practical* dimension. After all, we don't need to be experts in theology to face the implications of a divine sorrow: it's enough that we know that everything we can imagine falls short. In any case, if we meditate on it, it's not hard to burst into *thanksgiving* before a God who, in want of nothing, makes himself so vulnerable by creating us out of love. And from gratitude, we move on to filial *compassion* for this most loving Father on whom we bring so much hurt with the disasters in which our sins entangle us.

Nobody is so compassionate with that *sorrow of divine love* as Jesus Christ, who remedies it with the *sorrow of human love*

20 Benedict XVI, Encyclical on Christian Hope *Spe Salvi* (November 30. 2007), no. 39. Vatican website: www.vatican.va. See also Benedict XVI, Encyclical on Christian Love *Deus Caritas Est* (December 25, 2005), nos. 9–10. Vatican website: www.vatican.va. The Holy Father affirms that God's love is not only *agape* but also in a certain sense *eros*: that is "the love that unites the free gift of oneself with the impassioned desire for reciprocity." Message for Lent 2007.

of his heart: his harmony with God the Father is unrivaled. That is the first motive behind the plan of Redemption: the Son *consoles* the Father for all the offenses he receives because of our indifference. We can't grasp what an infinite being experiences, but the incarnate Word makes it accessible to us. In particular, the Passion reveals to us the magnitude of both divine love and divine *sorrow*: Jesus as our Head wanted to make reparation to God the Father, and he did so by suffering as much as possible so that we would be able to glimpse how much each sin *affects* the Father. If we're good sons and daughters, it will give us joy to know that the Father, for centuries now, has been receiving the best of all consolations. However, we will feel more uneasy if we realize the burden that this entails for Jesus' heart, if we discover that he offers not only the *physical pain* of his bloody Passion but also the *inner pain* that our sins inflict on him. We will feel, in summary, the urgency of co-redeeming with Christ, of alleviating his burdens with which he consoles the Father and obtains for us the saving grace of the Holy Spirit.

The First Sin and Its Consequences

The need for the Redemption dates back to the dawn of history. The first chapters of the Book of Genesis, without being strictly historical, recount that God treated Adam and Eve as some earthly parents treat their children. He gave them the best environment and the best education. They lived in an idyllic place and enjoyed the love and continued intimacy of the one who, with all trust, they called Father. He obtained for them the best gifts, both natural (a sharp intelligence, strong will, and perfectly ordered passions) and supernatural (the *state of grace* that gave them the status of children of God). They suffered no physical pain because they had also received certain exceptional qualities (preternatural gifts). They didn't even have to die: when their happy days on earth were done, they would pass on painlessly to the other life. Everything was elaborately arranged to prevent them from leaving their path. But they still had the use of their freedom, and, although they could only sin out of pride, they did!

The devil, the most cunning expert in deception and disinformation, disguising himself as someone who was not at war with God, successfully planted in them a doubt about the divine intentions. Shrewdly, he begins his attack asking the woman, "Did God say, 'You shall not eat of any tree of the garden'?" (Gn 3:1). Her attention captured, he suggests that the divine threat couldn't be real—that all would not be lost—that although the Creator had said he wanted to be their Father, he was really trying to turn them into slaves. He twists the Creator's intentions, "placing in doubt the truth about God, who is love, and leaving man only with a sense of the master–slave relationship. As a result, the Lord appears jealous of his power over the world and over man."[21]

The fall of the earth's first inhabitants must have been something dramatic. They entered into contention with God, who had asked them to keep just one commandment: not to eat of the tree of "the knowledge of good and evil" (Gn 2:17). That single restriction was imposed on them for their own good: so that they would escape self-sufficiency: if they would let themselves be loved by God, they would receive everything they needed, but if they disobeyed, the consequences would be catastrophic. They would grieve their Father immensely; they would lose all their supernatural and preternatural gifts; they would harm themselves irremediably and would pass this lamentable condition on to their descendants. And so it was! For this reason, we arrive in the world with a *fallen nature*, as "has-beens." God created us to be happy, loving as he loves, but our nature has deteriorated because of the dead weight with which that original sin has left us. We miss our lost dignity. We search for it ceaselessly, but seldom in the right places. You might say the pride that provoked the original fall has settled down within us. Original sin, then, is a "real but obscure datum" which offers us "truly the key for interpreting reality."[22] If God had not revealed it to us,

---

21 St. John Paul II, *Crossing the Threshold of Hope*, p. 228.
22 St. John Paul II, *Crossing the Threshold of Hope*, p. 228.

we wouldn't have discovered its existence by reason alone, although there are clues that would have allowed us to suspect it.[23] We're like eagles unable to rise in flight because of an old injury. We harbor high ideals, but, at the moment of truth, our deeds make our weakness undeniable.

In any case, it would be a little too convenient to throw all the blame on original sin. Our nature has continued to deteriorate because of later sins, although none will be as lucid as the first. In our inherited predicament, there is always a certain dose of ignorance and weakness in our own sins. Thus, no sin in the present will be as blameworthy as that of our first parents. That one is similar to the sin of the fallen angels, those creatures of great perfection whose sin of pride transformed them into essentially and irremediably malignant beings. But there's one great difference: no matter how perfect Adam and Eve were, they were still human, and thus, they could repent, ask forgiveness, and be saved.

Faced with the terrible consequences of the first sin, the question inevitably arises: Why didn't God just wipe the slate clean and start over? Wouldn't that have been the

23 According to St. Thomas Aquinas, it can be proved with sufficient probability (*Summa contra Gentiles* 4.52). It's like a puzzle that's missing a single piece, and once it's found, everything falls into place. John Henry Newman, canonized in 2019, takes the example of a young beggar whom we notice, upon close observation, has the gestures of someone born into a prosperous family. All signs point to some kind of calamity in early childhood (see his *Apologia pro vita sua*).

best way to avoid so much subsequent misery? The fact that he didn't do so confirms something we've already guessed: we're not "remote control marionettes," and God is always consistent about respecting our autonomy *down to its ultimate consequences.* If, for example, someone shoots an innocent person, God doesn't stop the bullet. If he treated us like irresponsible children, we would never learn to take our freedom seriously. Refraining from coercion entails a respect for all its implications as well.

God has acted like the best of earthly fathers. With these, if one of their children gets in trouble, without ceasing to respect the child's freedom, they do anything they can to help. If a child had an incurable illness, they would spare no sacrifice to seek out a cure. Or if the child became a drug addict and there was no place for his rehabilitation, they would build one themselves. God has acted in the same way. When his children were harmed by the contagion of the consequences of sin, he set in motion a wonderful plan of Redemption which culminated in the death on the Cross of his only begotten Son, the new Adam, with the priceless help of Mary, the new Eve.

The solution that God devised and put into practice is doubtless the best possible one: it restores things after the first sin without attacking the imperatives of freedom. Far from falling out with the sinner, his compassion leads him to seek a solution. St. John Paul II notes that it is one and the same love that inspires both Creation and the plan of Redemption: "this inscrutable and indescribable fatherly 'pain' will bring about above all the wonderful economy of redemptive love in Jesus Christ."[24] That design continues to respect our freedom scrupulously. On the Cross, Jesus obtains for us a medicine able to cure all our illnesses, but he does not by any means oblige us to take it.

In conclusion, if, even knowing how much we could twist it, God decided to give his creative *fiat*, this was because his eternal design already contemplated the future Incarnation with a view to the Redemption. He knew that he could set right what had been bent and, at the same time, by becoming man, make it easier for us to respond to his love. Before addressing the urgency of consoling his Sacred Heart, as a sort of bridge, let us take some time to look at one of the most ancient devotions in the life of the Church.

---

24   St. John Paul II, *Dominum et Vivificantem*, no. 39.

CHAPTER 7

Devotion to the Sacred Heart Of Jesus

Catholic Piety

The classic term that designates familiarity with God is *piety*. It's significant that this word is related to a loving compassion. In antiquity, it indicated the compassionate attitude of children toward their parents, generally when they were old. In the Christian sense, someone who is accustomed to relation with God marked by a great ease, simplicity, and affection is *pious*. Through the divine initiative, by means of certain private revelations, or to imitate the saints' example, the *life of piety* in the Church has crystallized into certain public or private devotions. We see, for example, acts of adoration of Jesus Christ in the Blessed Sacrament, or the recitation of the Holy Rosary to the Virgin Mary. The essential thing is still personal prayer, but that list of devotions helps to channel the desire to praise God and venerate the saints.

Among these *pious practices*, the devotion to the *Sacred Heart of Jesus* stands out. It is an inheritance of centuries that helps direct the Christian's compassion for the pains that afflict the heart of the Redeemer. In particular, it channels the desire to make up for the ingratitude and affronts he receives. As Pius XI affirmed in 1928, "we can and ought to console that Most Sacred Heart which is continually wounded by the sins of thankless men."[1] Alluding to the "sorrow" of God, Benedict XVI indicates that "[n]ot surprisingly, many of the saints found in the Heart of Jesus the deepest expression of this mystery of love."[2] A look at the history of this devotion, then, is always an excellent opportunity to learn from the example of so many saints who have lived it out.

The Catholic Faith does not oblige us to believe in apparitions or private revelations, but only in what has been revealed by God: the contents of the Bible and Tradition (not everything that Jesus said is contained in the Gospel—see Jn 21:25) and what has been confirmed by the Church's magisterium. In the same way, all Catholics are free to choose the pious practices they find most helpful or most suited to their sensibilities. The Church, concretizing the third commandment of the Decalogue, obliges us to attend Mass on Sundays. But she does not impose any particular

---

1   Pius XI, Encyclical on Reparation to the Sacred Heart *Miserentissimus Redemptor* (May 8, 1928), no. 13. Vatican website: www.vatican.va.

2   Benedict XVI, Message for Lent 2007.

devotion or a trip to any Marian sanctuary. Still, it is good not to exclude other channels that the Lord has used to communicate himself to us, even more if they are approved by Church authority. The Sacred Heart devotion is the result of a progressive realization on the part of Catholics of the riches of Christ's love contained in the Faith. The Church's circumspect attitude regarding private revelations is manifest in the constant indications of the popes that this devotion doesn't add anything to what is derived from revealed truth. According to St. John Paul II, "the essential elements of this devotion belong in a *permanent* way to the Church's spirituality throughout her entire history."[3]

St. Margaret Mary Alacoque

The devotion to the Sacred Heart extended through the whole Catholic world after the private revelations to St. Mary Margaret Alacoque in Paray-le-Monial (France) became known. Between 1673 and 1675, this "nun of a gray appearance, always ill, very shy, timorous, and awkward"[4] had four visions in which she was taught about the heart of Christ as a symbol of his love and his humanity. Although the "learned people" of the area ruled that it was an illusion

3   St. John Paul II to the Superior General of the Society of Jesus, Paray-le-Monial, October 5, 1986.

4   Carlos Pujol, *La casa de los santos*, 2nd ed. (Madrid: Ediciones Rialp, 1991), p. 345.

not worthy of attention, the arrival at the convent of St. Claude la Colombière changed matters. The saint's support was decisive for St. Margaret Mary being able to overcome all those trials. The patience and spirit of humility with which she confronted so many misunderstandings by good people are striking. She was finally canonized in 1920, which upheld, more than two hundred years after her death, the message that she had known how to live and communicate in her own time.

To this saint, Jesus expressed his ardent desire of reparation for the offenses and ingratitude that he receives, especially where he manifests his love most: in the Eucharist. On December 27, 1673, the Lord told her that he had a "heart so full of passion with love for men, which, not being able to contain in itself any longer the flames of his burning charity, he must spread them through you." To make atonement for the offenses that the Eucharist receives, Jesus asked the French saint to promote frequent communion, above all on the first Fridays of each month, with a sense of reparation. This custom has been kept on first Fridays in many places to atone to the Lord with a Mass or by praying the litanies of the Sacred Heart.

The generosity of St. Margaret Mary and her closeness to the heart of Jesus burst into a madness of love that reaches unsuspected heights: I suffer so little, she says, "that what makes me suffer the most is that I don't suffer enough."[5] Any quantity of sacrifice appears too little to her, because she feels the urgency of co-redeeming with Christ. Thus, she writes,

> We cannot love the Lord if we do not suffer for him. Nothing in this world is capable of pleasing me except the Cross of my divine Master, a Cross like his, heavy and ignominious, without sweetness, consolation, or relief. Let others have the luck to accompany my divine Savior in his ascent to Mount Tabor; for my part, I do not desire to know any other path than the one that leads to Calvary, because nothing that is not the Cross appeals to me in the least. My destiny will be, then, to be on Calvary until my last sign of life, in the midst of the insults, the thorns, the nails, and the Cross, with no other consolation or pleasure than that of not having any. And what happiness to be able to suffer in silence always![6]

To make clear that the devotion to the Sacred Heart is not merely an invention of a seventeenth-century saint, the Church insists that it already existed earlier. In fact, in France, the Solemn Feast of the Heart of Jesus was celebrated for the first time on October 20, 1672, when St. Margaret Mary

---

5   John Croiset, *The Devotion to the Sacred Heart of Jesus* (Rockford, IL: TAN, 1988), p. 14.

6   Croiset, p. 13.

was only twenty-five years old. As Pius XII emphasizes, this devotion has not "suddenly appeared in the Church; rather, it has blossomed forth of its own accord as a result of that lively faith and burning devotion of men who were endowed with heavenly gifts, and who were drawn towards the adorable Redeemer and his glorious wounds which they saw as irresistible proofs of that unbounded love."[7]

Historical Overview

Devotion to the Sacred Heart started on the basis of the meditation of one fact that marked Christ's Passion: a soldier pierced Jesus' side to make certain he had already died. The evangelist who records it recalls an Old Testament passage in which the prophet Zechariah foretells, "They shall look on him whom they have pierced" (Jn 19:37).[8] The saints of the first centuries, from Justin in the second century onward, reflected on the profound significance of that event. Up until the ninth century, the accent fell on the wound in Christ's side. Between the ninth and the twelfth centuries, the devotion began gradually to move from his open *side* to the wound of the heart pierced by the lance.

Among the saints who already lived out this devotion in a private way before the seventeenth century, Pius XII

---

7   Pius XII, Encyclical on Devotion to the Sacred Heart *Haurietis Aquas* (May 15, 1956), no. 96. Vatican website: www.vatican.va.

8   See also Zec 12:10.

names the following: St. Bonaventure, St. Albert the Great, St. Gertrude, St. Catherine of Siena, Bl. Henry Suso, St. Peter Canisius, St. Francis de Sales, and St. John Eudes.[9] One of the most relevant "precursors," in the twelfth century, was St. Bernard, who insisted on the importance of pouring out all our affection in our dealings with the Lord. According to him, the wounded heart of Christ reveals to us his infinite divine love, and his wounds are like a clamor that urges us to respond to his love.[10] His disciple, St. Lutgarde of Aywières (1182–1246) also emphasized the urgent need to soothe these wounds. A contemporary of hers tells how this Flemish holy woman heard from Jesus these words: "Pay attention, my beloved, to the cries that my wounds address to you, so that my blood should not be spilled in vain and my death not be futile."[11]

The edifying biography of St. Lutgarde illustrates how the devotion to the Sacred Heart is not a pure invention of sixteenth-century Spanish mystics or of the later seventeenth-century French school of spirituality. This saint's history is similar to so many who, from a very early age, sense the love of Christ. Unlike St. Margaret Mary of Alacoque, it seems that the young Lutgarde was very attractive and had many

9   See Pius XII, *Haurietis Aquas*.

10 See *vicem rependere* (correspondence) of St. Bernard in *Canticle of Canticles*, sermon 83, 4.

11 van Bellingen, *Vita Lutgardis*, 6.

admirers. When she was fifteen, just at the moment when she was to meet with one of them, her biography recounts how Christ appeared to her and, showing her the bleeding wound in his side, said to her, "Stop seeking the weaknesses of vain love. Look here and contemplate from now on what you ought to love and why: I assure you that from there you will obtain the purest delights." From then on, she grew so much in her love for Christ that "possessed by the desire to see Christ, she could spill rivers of tears."[12] The passionate Lutgarde learned from the Lord to refine her affections to the point of transforming them into what she called "a tranquil fervor." When it was difficult for her to moderate them, she used to ask the Lord for an *exchange of hearts*: that he would give her the grace to love with his Sacred Heart. It seems that one day when the Lord asked her what she wished for, she replied: "What I want is your heart." Jesus, in his turn, told her, "Rather, I am the one who is asking you for your heart." This confirmed, then, the reciprocity that exists in our relationship with Jesus Christ.

In essence, Christ asked St. Lutgarde to consecrate herself to his heart and make reparation for sins. He pressed her to co-redeem with him, uniting herself, with a true priestly soul, to the sacrifice of the Cross, renewed daily in the Holy Mass. According to her biography, in one of her visions, she

12   van Bellingen , 3, 9.

contemplated Jesus before God the Father, entreating him for the cause of sinners; later, he told her, "You see how I am offering myself entirely to the Father for sinners. I want you also to offer yourself to me for my sinners." Almost every day, during the Mass, the Lord repeated these same words.

Let's continue our historical overview. In the thirteenth century, three theologians reflected on the Sacred Heart: St. Albert the Great, St. Thomas Aquinas, and St. Bonaventure. The latter, a delicate and contemplative soul, meditating on the open side of Christ, wondered,

> Who will not love a heart so wounded? Who will not embrace a heart so pure? We, who are of flesh, will pay love with love, we will embrace our wound which the impious have pierced, hands and feet, the side and the heart. We beg to be worthy to bind our heart with the bond of his love and wound it with a lance, because it remains hard and impenitent.[13]

In the thirteenth century, three Central European religious women had revelations about the heart of Jesus: Mechthild of Magdeburg, Gertrude of Helfta, and Matilda of Hackeborn. St. Gertrude had a great impact in the Middle Ages. "In the heart of Gertrude you will find me," Christ had told her. Lope de Vega composed these verses in her honor: "You are

---

13   St. Bonaventure, *Vitis Mystica*, 3, 11, PL 32, 66.

the guardian while you enjoy the earth, and since all of God is hidden within you, your heart is better than heaven."[14]

In the middle of the fourteenth century, the Lord had explained to St. Catherine of Siena why he had allowed the lance to open his heart: so that we would understand that, as God, he loves us infinitely more than what he could show with his limited physical suffering. This doctor of the Church completed the intuition of St. Bernard, according to which what is human in Jesus Christ reveals what is divine: the visible wound of his heart is the gate that opens to his invisible divine love.

As early as the seventeenth century, St. John Eudes referred not only to the vulnerability of Jesus' heart but also to his capacity to rejoice. Thus, a merely "sorrow-ist" vision of Christian reparation is overcome: the best way to relieve Christ's pain is to offer him joys. This French saint was the first to draw attention to the close union that has existed for twenty centuries between the Sacred Heart of Jesus and the Immaculate Heart of Mary. St. Bernard and St. Gertrude had already recommended devotion to the heart of Mary, but Eudes underlines the affective co-penetration between those two hearts. To reinforce it, omitting the plural, he expressed the singular form, "*The* heart of Jesus and Mary."

14   As quoted in Pujol, p. 381; see also Benedict XVI, General Audience (October 6, 2010). Vatican website: www.vatican.va.

He used this prayer: "Heart of Jesus, which livest in and through Mary, Heart of Mary which livest in and for Jesus." In 1648, he composed a Mass in honor of the Heart of Mary, which he himself celebrated for the first time.

In the last three centuries, devotion to the Sacred Heart has nourished the piety of millions of Catholics. Since the twentieth century, it has had as a complement the devotion to the *merciful love*, which was born in France, above all on the basis of the teachings of St. Thérèse of Lisieux, and in Poland through St. Faustina Kowalska. The adjective *merciful* usually completes an ancient invocation to Jesus; now we say, "Most Sacred and merciful Heart, grant us peace." In the year 2000, upon the canonization of St. Faustina, St. John Paul II decided that every second Sunday of Easter would be celebrated in the entire Church as the Feast of Divine Mercy.[15] Thus, we are urged to spread that devotion, to pray for sinners, and to learn to conduct ourselves mercifully with our fellow men and women.[16]

The Immaculate Heart of Mary

The devotions to the Sacred Heart of Jesus and the Immaculate Heart of Mary are parallel and inseparable, as

---

15   The dates of the death (2005) and beatification (2011) are linked to the day on which this feast is celebrated.

16   Michel Esparza, *Amor y autoestima* [Self-esteem without selfishness] (Madrid: Ediciones Rialp, 2012), pp. 237–240.

are their missions in earthly life as well as in glory.[17] Both have a glorified body, and, from heaven, contemplate, in a vigil of love, all the good and evil that we do. They will not be at ease until the end of time. From Golgotha until the Parousia, no one relieves the burdens of Jesus' Heart as she does, or offers him so many joys. In this way, she helps her Son to give rise to the life of grace in us.

That intimate affective union can be traced back to the moment in which Mary conceived Jesus in her womb. Ever since the physical heart of her Son began to develop a few inches from his mother's, both hearts beat in unison and share all the joys and sorrows that we procure for them. "A bond: a splendid union of hearts!"[18] It is the *admirable alliance* of those who love one another both humanly and divinely. On the one hand, Jesus showers his mother with his immense divine gifts and with his passionate filial love. On the other, "for Mary, Christ will always be God as well as man. He will always be the one who gives her everything, as well as the one who needs to receive something."[19] And she is the one who gives the most, the one most closely associated with the task of Redemption.

17   See St. John Paul II, Encylical *Redemptor Hominis* (March 4, 1979), no. 22. Vatican website: www.vatican.va.

18   St. John Paul II, Angelus (June 30, 1985), no. 2. Vatican website: www. vatican.va.

19   Santiago Martín, *El Evangelio secreto de la Virgen María* (Barcelona: Planeta, 1996), pp. 263–264.

That bond between the two was definitively sealed on Calvary. There was realized "the definitive alliance of the Hearts, the Mother's and the Son's."[20] No one lightens Jesus' Cross the way Mary does. Therefore, she wanted to stay so close to him. That was the divine plan for her, long meditated, ever since Simeon announced that a sword would pierce her Heart (see Lk 2:35). She was the only one to understand fully why it was good for her Son to be sacrificed. The apostles, though they had been chosen by Christ, didn't understand it, whereas she, with her priestly soul, wished to be beside the Cross for three reasons: to sustain her Son, to console the Father, and in him, to obtain saving grace.

Ever since she agreed to be associated with the redemptive sacrifice, she became our mother. When Jesus on the Cross delivered her up to us through John (see Jn 19:26–27), Jesus didn't constitute her motherhood but declared it. Since then, she has not ceased to draw us close to her Son. With St. John Paul II, we can ask her, "Mary, Mother of mercy, show your children the Heart of Jesus, which you saw opened to be always a fount of life."[21]

It's enlightening to run through the little history of the devotion to the Heart of Mary as well. Two centuries after St. John Eudes showed us the affective co-penetration

---

20 St. John Paul II, Angelus (September 15, 1985), no. 4.
21 St. John Paul II, Address in Paray-le-Monial (October 5, 1985).

between Mary's Heart and that of her Son, the veneration of both became the common patrimony of all Catholics in the wake of Mary's petition in 1830 to St. Catherine Labouré to mint the "miraculous medal." On it, there appear imprinted twelve stars surrounding two hearts.[22]

In the twentieth century, the apparitions of the Virgin of Fatima made clear that to console the heart of the mother is to console the heart of the Son, and vice versa. Mary urged three little shepherd children, Lucia, Francisco, and Jacinta, to co-redeem with her Son: to offer little sacrifices to console him and help him to save sinners. In the last apparition, on October 13, 1917, one detail reveals their intimate communion. The Mother of Christ, "taking on a sadder expression," said: "Do not offend my Son any more; he is already very much affected." The afflicted countenance of Mary must have been striking: Lucia commented that she would never forget the sorrow she saw in this most tender of mothers.[23]

In 1925, Mary and Jesus appeared to Lucia. On that occasion, Jesus, pointing to the heart of Mary, which appeared surrounded by thorns, exhorted the seer of Fatima to "have compassion on that heart, continually martyred by

22   The same stars that inspired the emblem and flag of the European Council. That emblem was also adopted later in 1985 by the European Union.
23   As quoted in Pier Liugi Zampetti, *La profecía de Fátima* (Madrid: Ediciones Rialp, 1992), pp. 129, 133.

human ingratitude, without anyone to console it with acts of atonement." The Virgin added, "Look, my daughter, at my heart, surrounded by thorns, with which ungrateful men pierce it at every moment with their blasphemies and ingratitude. You, at least, try to console me."[24] Concretely, our mother asked for atonement especially on the first Saturdays of five successive months, with recourse to confession and Communion, praying the Rosary and contemplating its mysteries. What good son would not feel his own heart break if he found his mother's was surrounded by thorns? Everything would seem little to console her, not only a few Saturdays of the year, but every day.

In conclusion, the heart of Jesus reveals to us the divine love, and "*through the heart of the Mother we discover the love of the Savior.*" These words are the title of a message addressed by St. John Paul II to the participants in an international symposium celebrated in Fatima in 1986 on the relation between the two hearts. "Our devotion to Mary's Immaculate Heart expresses our reverence for her maternal compassion both for Jesus and for all of us her spiritual children."[25]

---

24   As quoted in Chanoine Barthas, *La Virgen de Fátima*, 9th ed. (Madrid: Ediciones Rialp, 1991), pp. 545–546.

25   St. John Paul II, Address to the Participants of the International Symposium on the Alliance of the Hearts of Jesus and Mary (September 22, 1986), no. 2. Vatican website: www.vatican.va.

Hopeful Horizon

Are those devotions in crisis? Why? As we have seen, they will always be relevant, being rooted in the essence of the Christian life. "[They] have led," said St. Josemaría in 1966, "and still [lead] to conversion, self-giving, fulfilment of God's will and a loving understanding of the mysteries of the redemption."[26] In those years, unfortunately, a notable decline began in all devotions, due to a crisis in the Church that arose around the Second Vatican Council. In 1986, St. John Paul II confirmed that those devotions were still relevant when he remarked, "it is a question of spiritual paths still worth offering to believers today."[27] But few paid attention.

Those difficult times, which usually appear—as at other moments in history—after a major council, were compounded due to a cultural atmosphere that encouraged questioning everything old simply for being old, without offering alternatives. Believing that everything needs to be changed denotes a naive and presumptuous attitude. Mature people manage to combine *fidelity* to the legacy received with the *creativity* to adapt it to new cultural contexts. Thus they allow perennial truths to be lived out in the most varied circumstances. That's why *innovations* are necessary: they

26   Escrivá, *Christ Is Passing By*, no. 163.
27   St. John Paul II to Fr. Peter-Hans Kolvenbach, October 5, 1986.

serve to renew what is outworn, to revitalize what is already stagnant. *Revolutions*, on the other hand, tend to wreak havoc.

No doubt during our own lifetimes we lack historical perspective. Still, the crisis the Church has been suffering since the 1960s is perhaps one of the most serious of its history. People are questioning not only the old devotions, but also each and every one of the truths of faith and morals. At any rate, despite all our wretchedness, Christ, as he promised, keeps guiding the *barque of Peter* and brings it to safe harbor even in the midst of the most terrible storms. St. Paul VI, St. John Paul II, and Benedict XVI have weathered many storms, with the waters now returning to their courses. The trouble is that, as a result of this crisis, the lack of formation of two-thirds of the baptized is glaring. For those who grew up in Europe, it is common to see statues or images of the Sacred Heart carved into the doors of old houses. However, due to this lack of formation, few today understand their meaning.

The reason for the decline in the devotion of the Sacred Heart lies not only in the post-Vatican II crisis. Already, earlier what began as an invitation to respond to the love of Christ had degenerated into a series of *stereotypical practices* with which the Catholic could be assured of divine protection. There were songs and laminated figures of the Sacred Heart that could never inspire devotion in any person of common sense. Many images of devotion parade an impoverished sentimentalism.

Nevertheless, "it is bad logic to turn these particular abuses—which are disappearing anyway—into some sort of doctrinal, theological problem."[28] The same thing happened with the popular devotion to the Sacred Heart as with the Holy Week processions. They are a magnificent opportunity to do penance and express loving compassion for the redemptive sufferings of Christ. Some, however, were quite critical of these manifestations of popular religiosity. It would be more positive to foster real piety by means of a good religious formation on co-redemption with Christ and the meaning of works of penitence. When popular devotion becomes distorted, the solution is to renew it, not eliminate it.

In the devotion to the Sacred Heart, concretely, experience has confirmed the negative effect of all that futile criticism. Something a vice rector of the Catholic University of Louvain said in a homily about the loss of *piety* among Catholics serves as an example:

> Jesus is sensitive, because being sensitive is a quality, and now that he's glorified for all time, Jesus continues to be sensitive . . . . Our generation doesn't know anymore how to console Christ as the Flemish mystics did in their day. We've become

28   Escrivá, *Christ Is Passing By*, no. 163.

> allergic to meditation on the *Via Crucis* and all forms
> of compassion for Jesus. We've grown impoverished;
> we have lost our most beautiful traditions, and with
> them . . . our hearts.[29]

After the passivity of the last few decades, it's urgent to
rediscover this devotion. It's a matter, in the end, of valuing
with new gusto the most essential thing in Christianity—
the love of Christ for each one of us—and to draw out its
practical consequences: to atone with deeds of love for "the
immense suffering and anguish of Christ at not seeing his
love requited by men."[30] We can never meditate enough
on the consequences of Christ's Passion. In 2010, before
the Holy Shroud of Turin, Benedict XVI commented that
"Every trace of blood speaks of love and of life. Especially
that huge stain near his rib, made by the blood and water
that flowed copiously from a great wound inflicted by the
tip of a Roman spear. That blood and that water speak of
life. It is like a spring that murmurs in the silence."[31]

---

29 As quoted in *Monsignore . . . ma non troppo: Hommage à Monseigneur Joseph Devroede (1915–1989)* (Louvaine: Peeters, 1991), p. 181.

30 Pich, pp. 61–62.

31 Benedict XVI, Meditation (May 2, 2010). Vatican website: www.vatican.va.

Chapter 8

Compassion for the Sorrowful Heart of Christ

A Little-Known Reality

Few are the Christians who realize how much they can offer to the Sacred Heart. If they hear talk of Christ's pain, they're aware of how much he suffered during the Passion, but they reason that now that he's in heaven, nothing disturbs him. They don't realize that, as Pius XI noted, "even now, in a wondrous yet true manner, we can and ought to console that Most Sacred Heart which is continually wounded by the sins of thankless men."[1]

In how we approach the pain of God, it is understandable that people are startled when they hear of the sufferings the

---

1   Pius XI, *Miserentissimus Redemptor*, no. 13.

glorious Christ suffers in the present. We have always been taught that in heaven, people don't suffer, that the souls of the blessed enjoy perfect felicity. This being the case, why does the glorious soul of Christ "suffer"? Because Jesus and Mary, until the end of time, live out, with loving closeness to us all. the vicissitudes of those on earth. In any case, it's a kind of "suffering" that is compatible with the happiness of heaven.

Being in tune with the burdens of the heart of the risen Jesus Christ doesn't require us to be experts in theology. Common sense tells us that those who are in heaven have nothing to worry about. But if what we do on earth didn't affect him, or God the Father, only two possibilities would remain: either they don't know what's happening down here, or they don't care.

Both alternatives are equally absurd, because they would amount to a limit improper to their power, or an indifference manifestly incompatible with their love. For the rest, it has now become clear again that the feelings of the heart of Jesus have not changed since his Ascension into heaven. We know that all our concerns affect him to the degree that he loves us. Love always entails an increase in vulnerability and the capacity to rejoice. Affection leads to the identification with the joys and pains of the beloved. Everyone who loves, including the most perfect man, exposes himself to sufferings and joys. Depending on whether his love is requited or not, he experiences happiness or grief, gratitude or disappointment.

Underlining the union of Christ with men, St. Josemaría affirms, "And now the same Christ is suffering in his members, in all of humanity spread throughout the earth, whose head and firstborn and redeemer he is."[2] Certainly, the present burdens on the heart of Jesus are derived from his loving identification with each one of us. There is no sorrow or joy on earth that he does not share. In particular, our troubles, especially the harm that each sin causes us, hurt him to the extent that he loves us. His redemptive sufferings are not only tied to his identification with us, but also to his love for God the Father. We've already seen that the Creator "has made himself vulnerable,"[3] and that Jesus, in his Passion, reveals to us the magnitude of divine *sorrow* at the same time as he teaches us how to relieve it.

In the end, what spurs our generosity most is the joy that our love procures for the sorrowing heart of Jesus. Nothing incites our response to his love like the *compassion* we feel upon realizing how much he suffers because of our sins. A child who, in a catechism class, had been told of the sorrow that Jesus experiences in heaven because of our sins, said, "Now Jesus can't bleed anymore, but he can still cry."

---

2   Escrivá, *Christ Is Passing By*, no. 168.
3   Joseph Ratzinger, *Jesus of Nazareth,* vol. 1 (New York: Image, 2007), p. 178.

Continuing with this way of speaking, childlike but close to the truth, we observe that this "crying" is heart-rending because it doesn't proceed from a superficial sensitivity but out of the depths of a loving and wounded heart. If we perceive his *tears*, we are moved and feel urged to console him. The imperious desire to alleviate his sadness takes us out of ourselves. Our problems look like insignificant *scratches* in comparison with his *wounds*.

That reaction to the suffering of another doesn't only shake big-hearted people. Even the most egotistical person, witnessing a serious traffic accident and seeing the driver, a perfect stranger, bleeding on the ground, feels urged to help. How, then, will those who don't know of the sufferings of his heart love the Lord, if, in practice, they think that they can't offer him anything? What would St. Teresa of Kolkata have done, for example, if the Lord had not made her understand his *thirst* to receive her love?

It's a shame that so many Christians are ignorant of that reality, even more if we consider that the practical consequences of this are far from trivial. Might this not be the reason that so many Catholics don't live, in practice, that loving union with Christ? They limit themselves to routine fulfillment of their religious obligations but don't acquire a deep interior life. They get married in the Church, they baptize their children, and, to set them a good example, they attend Holy Mass every Sunday. But in that kind of "social Catholicism," what's lacking is life. Maybe they'd be surprised if we asked them, "Do you think that Jesus misses you if you don't accompany him a little while near the tabernacle?"

The lack of affective harmony with Christ is even more painful when seen in those who have committed their life to a celibate apostolate. If the love of the Lord doesn't inspire their efforts, all that remains is their sacrificing themselves for love of an ideal: for example, promoting some work of charity or apostolate. But loving an ideal and loving a person are not the same thing. In this, as in all things, nature doesn't forgive. If love of Christ doesn't give life to the efforts of those who have given him everything, their devotion will probably lose its power, as in any marriage in which the relations between the spouses erode: instead of forming a close family, they end up resembling a corporate enterprise. Sometimes, with the passing of time, human attachments appear which put their fidelity at risk. And among those who manage to persevere in their commitment, some—the more half-hearted ones—do it by minimizing their devotion; others, who are trying harder, end up suffocated by that voluntarism that has its roots in pride. In either case, they're not very happy.

It's worth insisting, then, on the great power we have over the sorrowing and grateful heart of Jesus: it would be an injustice to neglect this, since it can be a spur to our response, and because the most obvious is sometimes the least often noticed and most often ignored.

The Christian Meaning of Suffering

What St. Edith Stein called the "science of the Cross" is a great mystery that becomes less obscure with the light offered by Christ's Passion. Broadly speaking, we can all identify with these words: "The meaning of sorrow is the consequence of our meaning of life. One can face that suffering when it's borne *for something or someone*. It is in love that it finds its meaning."[4] The most relevant question is knowing *why* and *for love of whom*.

These words of St. Josemaría capture Christian wisdom on this question: "What does suffering matter if we suffer to console, to please God our Lord, in a spirit of reparation, united to him on his Cross; in a word: if we suffer for Love?"[5] The lack of being in tune with the pained and grateful heart of Christ is a serious obstacle to living with depth the *Christian meaning of suffering*. After all, the terrible experience of suffering can present three advantages: an

4   Antonio Vázquez, *Juan Larrea: Un rayo de luz sobre fondo gris* (Madrid: Palabra, 2009), p. 33.

5   Escrivá, *The Way*, no. 182.

opportunity for purification, a point of encounter for abandoning ourselves trustingly to God, and an opportunity for co-redemption with Christ. It is in this last one that the greatest contribution of Christianity lies. The other two elements, purification and abandonment, comprise a great aid in the acceptance of suffering, but they turn out to be insufficient to love as Jesus does those who, as we have just seen, are identified with him.

Indeed, the wisdom of the ancient Greeks indicated the purifying value of contradictions, even from a merely human point of view. Moreover, as the Old Testament makes clear in the Book of Job, we know that our crosses, sometimes as unexpected as they are incomprehensible, offer us an excellent opportunity to abandon ourselves trustingly in a loving divine providence. The Christian perspective assumes and moves beyond these two insights, already present in Greek and Jewish wisdom. Thanks to that new vision revealed to us by Christ, we can discover in pain "not a heartless determinism, but the loving hand of our Father of Heaven, who blesses us with the loveable demands of the Cross."[6] It is urgent, then, to go deeper into the opportunity that all the baptized enjoy to transform our sufferings into an occasion

---

6   Bishop Javier Echevarría, Homily, University of Navarra, October 23, 2010; translated directly from the Spanish. See "Prelate's Homily at the University of Navarra: October 23, 2010," Opus Dei, https://multimedia.opusdei.org/pdf/en/3homily.pdf, for English version.

of co-redeeming with Christ, helping him to console God the Father and to save souls.

According to Church doctrine, we are called to participate and collaborate in the work of Redemption.[7] But, practically, what does this collaboration entail? What does it mean, as St. Peter indicates (see 1 Pt 3:14), that the Christian is called to share in his sufferings? In what sense can St. Paul claim that he makes up in his flesh "what is lacking in Christ's afflictions" (Col 1:24). In my last book, I attempted to respond to those questions,[8] wanting to show that our suffering can alleviate the sufferings that Christ offers to console the Father and save souls. In a strict sense, we cannot do anything today to make the flogging that Jesus received during the scourging at the pillar hurt any less. Nor can we help him carry the weight of the Cross on his way to Calvary as Simon of Cyrene did twenty centuries ago (see Mt 27:32).[9] On the other hand, we can lighten the suffering that our sins, happening in the present, cause him. For this reason, St. John Paul II puts it like this: "In this dimension— the dimension of love—the Redemption which has already

---

7   See St. Paul VI, Dogmatic Constitution on the Church *Lumen Gentium* (November 21, 1964), no. 62. Vatican website: www.vatican.va.

8   Esparza, *Self-Esteem without Selfishness*; in Spanish ed., *Amor y autoestima*, pp. 205–227.

9   See also Mk 15:21; Lk 23:26.

been completely accomplished is, in a certain sense, constantly being accomplished."[10]

In this case, I'll leave aside the theological ins and outs and confine myself to telling an anecdote. I still remember something a family man I know said in passing during a meal. It stayed in my memory, perhaps because it helped me understand that, when it comes to sacrificing ourselves for love of the Lord, we can be inspired just as we would for any human love. That good father had a very hard time getting up in the morning, because he worked late hours. Besides, ever since he was little, he had always found it hard to get up. His mind felt foggy every morning; to be in any condition to face another day, he needed several cups of coffee. However, when it came to his love for his children, without thinking anything of it at all, he would say with

10   St. John Paul II, Apostolic Letter on the Christian Meaning of Human Suffering *Salvifici Doloris* (February 11, 1984), no. 24. Vatican website: www.vatican.va. The classic explanation of the *actuality of the sufferings of Christ* rests on the way all his actions, since he is truly God, transcend the limits of time and space. Given that "all that he did and suffered for all men . . . participates in the divine eternity" (*Catechism*, no. 1085), we can, two thousand years later, truly change the weight of his Cross. But let's not forget that Jesus, besides being God, is also a man like us. Therefore, the actuality of his passion can also be explained with an eye to his human nature. Indeed, since his holy humanity looks upon us from heaven, it should be no surprise to learn that all the good and evil that happens on earth has its echo in his glorious heart. Certainly, the explanations linked to his divine nature offer greater theological security, but if we only focus on them, we run the risk of falling into that "practical monophysitism" that we mentioned in our review of Christology.

great conviction that *it was a real sacrifice for him not to get up at night when he heard one of his little children crying.*

This is how our nature "works." We don't generally spare any effort when it comes to easing the pain of those we love. Getting up in the middle of the night will never be pleasant, except in helping a child to recover from a nightmare. No sane person loves suffering as an *end* in itself. But sacrifice can be chosen with pleasure as a *means* of contributing to the happiness of someone we love. Only thus is it understandable that the saints can love pain despite the natural dread it produces. St. Josemaría, for instance, contends that suffering gives him "joy and peace," because he feels "so much desire for reparation": love made him "rejoice in suffering."[11] Jesus, too, in Gethsemane, felt "sorrowful and troubled" (Mt 26:37), but his love for the Father and for us gave him the strength necessary to undertake and consummate the Passion. If we imitate him, our suffering, too, will be made light. The Lord does not delight in our suffering as such: indeed, with empathy, he feels it as his own. He only wishes, for our own good, that we should love him. Our willing sacrifice consoles him to the degree that it's an expression of love.

Moreover, sacrificing for the good of another person makes us love that person more. In the end, that is one

---

11   As quoted in Andrés Vázquez de Prada, *The Founder of Opus Dei*, vol. 1 (New York: Scepter, 2001): "Lord, that I might see!"

of the reasons good parents love their children so much: because they've spent so many years taking compassion on their neediness and therefore sacrificing so much for them. At bottom, love and pain are two realities that benefit from one another. There is between them a sort of feedback mechanism. Love makes any sacrifice more bearable, and suffering to make someone we love happy brings us to love them even more.

This human truth takes on a much deeper meaning from the Christian point of view. "Love makes suffering fruitful and suffering deepens love."[12] Since sacrificial devotion is usually preceded by compassion, we also, like so many saints who have gone before us, will love the Lord madly if, when we meditate on his Passion, we *feel* his love and pain. Compassion for his sorrowing heart will be the best spur to our own generosity. For love of him, perhaps without *feeling like it* but with *pleasure*, we will go all out to fulfill with the greatest possible perfection the little duties of each instant.

The Urgency of Co-Redeeming with Christ

Throughout these pages, we have underscored that in the Christian life it's not a matter of trying to love the Lord simply because it will help us become better and ultimately be saved, but above all because the well-being of his vulnerable

12   St. John Paul II, Homily for the Canonization of Edith Stein (October 11, 1998), no. 7. Vatican website: www.vatican.va.

and grateful heart urges us on. This is what we should prize above all.

What helps us most to focus all our efforts on the love of Christ is the compassionate meditation on his Passion. He does not die on the Cross only to reveal to us the Father's *sorrow* but also to *console him*. The Redemption was not "invented" solely for our salvation, but above all so that Christ, as man, would be able to make up for the sins of all humanity for his Father. It was not only a matter of healing our wounds and showing us the way back to the Father's house, but also to ensure that the Father should receive from his incarnate Son all the love that his other children denied him. In some sense, then, it is not God the Father who "worries" us most, given that his consolation is already assured. The one about whom we should really feel uneasy is Jesus Christ, who, being the innocent only Son, consoles the Father for the sins that we, the truly guilty, commit. And he brings this work of loving reparation to completion by offering him immense physical and moral sufferings. And who helps him, besides his mother, to console the Father and obtain that grace from the Holy Spirit, which makes our sanctification possible?

The more generous we are for love of him, the lighter will be the weight of his Cross. There are two loves—for the Father and for souls—which motivate Christ's sacrifice. And just as there are in Mary, there are three loves that urge us to co-redeem: *through him* (Jesus), *with him* (God the Father), and *in him* (the souls). Relieving the burden of the heart of Jesus, we help him to console the Father and to save souls.

The work of the Redemption is a single process which, nonetheless, spans a long period of time. Twenty centuries ago, Jesus Christ was immolated in a bloody manner on the Cross, thus fulfilling God's salvific plan "once for all" (Heb 9:26).[13] Nonetheless, the Redemption will continue being completed until the end of the world. The *Paschal Mystery* of the death, Resurrection, and glorification of Christ will only be consummated with his glorious Second Coming, when he comes again to this world to judge the living and the dead (the *Parousia*). In his Passion, besides the *physical pains*, the Son offers to the Father great *interior sufferings*, many of which would be caused by the sins committed until the end of time.

The practical implications of these considerations are enormous for those of us who live in this *intermediate period*; those of us on earth before Christ comes in glory can lighten the weight that sins cause him as they happen. Since his human heart is interposed between God and us, we could say that Jesus redeems each new sin by means of a corresponding

13   See *Catechism*, no. 571 and its Compendium, *Compendium of the Catechism of the Catholic Church*, no. 112.

pain in his heart. As that child in catechism class said, he can't pour out his *blood* anymore, but he can pour out his *tears*. The moral suffering is perhaps worse than being crucified all over again. For sensitive people, a *broken heart* hurts more than a *broken bone*.

The possibility of mitigating the redemptive sufferings of Christ opens up for us a whole unsuspected horizon of compassionate reparation, which gives rise to ardent and effective desires to console him, loving him on behalf of those who don't love him. But in order really to feel the pressing urgency to co-redeem with him, each of us needs to face the *harsh reality*. Fortunately, or not, how much the Redeemer's Cross weighs depends on each one of us: according to whether we love him or sin against him, we can subtract from or add to its weight!

As the saying goes, "out of sight, out of mind." Thus the importance of trying to visualize the sorrows of our Savior, Jesus Christ. Practically, a few calculations may help reveal the magnitude of his sufferings. At this time, seven billion persons inhabit the earth. Every day, the Lord experiences, close up, the death of some one hundred and fifty thousand. To get an idea of the number of offenses the heart of Jesus is receiving presently, if one of each thousand inhabitants were to sin gravely, that would be seven million sins per day, some three hundred thousand per hour, five thousand per minute, and eighty per second! It's worth recalling this heartfelt consideration of St. Josemaría: "You must realize that Jesus is being offended constantly, and unfortunately, these offences are not being atoned for at the same rate."[14]

We could say that, as time passes, Jesus' pain at present sins increases, because more and more of us come into this world. Vittorio Messori, alluding to the number of the dead, says, "We are walking on the ashes of some three hundred billion living beings who have preceded us and that now, invisibly, are still there and will always be."[15] If this figure is correct, it's forty-three times the present world population. Only God knows how many human beings will pass through their time on earth until the end of time. The more time passes, the more people will have benefited from heaven, but, on the other hand, the greater will be the pain of the heart of the Redeemer. Compassion for him makes us desire the end of the world to come as soon as possible, since, as St. Augustine observes after recalling that the head of the Mystical Body is affected by the sufferings of each member, "there will be no definitive end of all his sufferings until the end of time has arrived."[16]

In any case, if we sense the magnitude of the wounds of the heart of Christ—in number and also in the intensity

---

14   Escrivá, *Furrow*, no. 480.

15   Messori, p. 217.

16   St. Augustine, *Enarrationes in Psalmos*, Ps 61:4; CCL 39, p. 373.

of the pain they produced—our hearts will burn with the desire to alleviate them, and we'll spare no effort to do so. Only then will everything we do for him seem little to us, unless there comes a day when we see that the love he receives outweighs the coldness. In the meantime, to rid him of the greatest burden possible, we'll go out of our way, seeking out new opportunities of surrender, while also trying to enhance the quality of the love that inspires our offerings.

On Golgotha, Mary, John, and a few women accompanied Jesus closely. Fortunately, there are many more of us to comfort him now. It wouldn't be excessive to compose an updated Way of the Cross that would allow us to channel our compassionate reparation. It would be a good way of consoling him throughout the *fourteen stations* that remind us of many other causes of the sadness of his heart. Here is a draft: 1) Eucharistic sacrileges and outrages; 2) disunity among Christians; 3) lukewarmness and infidelities to vocations; 4) blasphemies, idolatries, and superstitions; 5) indifferentism and religious persecution; 6) attacks against human life; 7) wars; 8) torture, emotional abuse, and physical aggression; 9) broken families; 10) hedonistic excess, rapes, human trafficking, abuse, and corruption of minors; 11) injustices against the most underprivileged and labor exploitation; 12) greed, fraud, and waste; 13) defamation, calumny, deception, tricks, and lies; 14) pride and its hatreds, rancors, envy, and disputes.

According to the happy expression of St. Josemaría, "Our Lord, with his arms outstretched"—that is, with a modest gesture of embracing us from the Cross—"is continually begging for your alms of love."[17] This means his thirst for love is continuous and he doesn't want us to feel in the least forced to satisfy it. He doesn't seek an external submission but an unconditional surrender. For this reason, when we're less generous with him, he doesn't throw it in our face. So as not to impose himself on us, he prefers to hide his disappointment, although, to the degree that our hearts start to be more in tune with his own, we begin to sense his silent requests.

Those who love with finesse try to avoid not only wounding but also disappointing their beloved. In any case, the Lord wants friends, not servants (see Jn 15:15). Rather than appealing to duty or justice, he desires free, loving belonging. In fact, he doesn't demand his *due* but awaits *gifts* offered with the generosity proper to love, the kind that express the surrender of what is most intimate: the will and the heart. The word *gift* is perhaps the best definition of the essence of love. As St. John Paul II contends, "To love means to give and to receive something which can be neither bought nor sold, but only given freely and mutually."[18]

17   Escrivá, *Forge*, no. 404.
18   St. John Paul II, Letter to Families *Gratissimam Sane* (February 2, 1994), no. 11. Vatican website: www.vatican.va.

It's something very personal between him and each one of us. It would be fitting, then, to bring it to our intimate conversation with him, and to ask him to have enough trust to show us the wounds of his heart (let's remember, just as an example, the countless abortions committed in the last few decades). If his pain becomes *palpable* to us and we decide to mitigate it with our *gifts*, our sacrifice will also have a positive side: it will be joyfully offered because our love for him will be greater than our suffering.[19] We already know that being affectively in tune always benefits both lover and beloved, since joys are increased when they are shared, whereas sorrows decrease. Therefore, we feel such happiness when we sense that our love is like an *ointment* to soothe his wounds. Nothing is so pleasant as to extract a smile from someone weeping disconsolately. Through the tears, that radiant smile shines like the sun piercing the clouds.

As a Paschal counterpoint to the Way of the Cross, we could also make a list of fourteen current motives for joy for the heart of Jesus. Besides sacrifices and good works, how a simple but sincere "I love you!" makes him rejoice. Sometimes, when it comes to love, we complicate things unnecessarily, forgetting that what is simplest but most sincere is usually the most welcome of all.

---

19 See St. Josemaría Escrivá, *The Way of the Cross*, the twelfth station (New York: Scepter, 1990), no. 3.

Everything From and To the Holy Mass

How can we channel daily "a vehement desire to live as co-redeemers with Christ"?[20] He himself gave us the best means of doing so when he instituted the Eucharist. Let us recall, as a sort of epilogue, the centrality the Holy Mass has in the Christian life. Here we face the mystery of faith *par excellence.* Like a compendium, it "binds together all the mysteries of Christianity."[21] There is no mystery revealed by Christ that is not present in each Eucharistic celebration. Its richness is such that we will never delve sufficiently deeply into the treasures it contains. Although we always fall short in our attempts to understand it, let us be truly grateful for this "invention which reveals the genius of that wisdom which is at the same time a madness of love."[22] In particular, the priests, who stand in the place of Christ, never get over their astonishment before "[t]his audacity of God who entrusts himself to human beings—who, conscious of our weaknesses, nonetheless considers men capable of acting and being present in his stead."[23]

"Take," Jesus Christ says to us in the first words of the consecration. He truly comes to the altar and asks us to *take*

---

20   Escrivá, *Christ Is Passing By*, no. 121.

21   Escrivá, *Conversations with Josemaría Escrivá* (New York: Scepter, 2002), no. 113.

22   Committee for Jubilee Year 2000, *La Eucaristía: Sacramento de vida nueva* (Madrid: BAC, 1999), p. 17.

23   Benedict XVI, Homily (June 11, 2010), during the Mass at the conclusion of the Year for Priests. Vatican website: www.vatican.va.

him, to receive him. He wants to offer himself up to each one of us and awaits us, even if we don't respond to his love,[24]at least to let ourselves be loved. In the Holy Mass, then, Christ's loving surrender coincides with our own. He instituted this sacrament to be able to renew daily his holocaust of love and for us to be able to join ourselves to his redemptive sacrifice.

Since the Eucharist means the culmination of the sacrifice of Christ, it makes sense that everything we do for love of him would have to move toward it. In every Eucharistic celebration, the Church—the priest together with each one of those in attendance—*offers himself to* Christ and *is offered with* Christ to the Father, to console him and to obtain the grace that saves souls.

The Eucharist is one of the Seven Sacraments instituted by Christ to make us participants in his redeeming grace. When they are celebrated, being sensible signs of invisible realities,[25] the most striking thing is what is not grasped by the senses. This is why it's so difficult for us to delve into the marvelous realities that only faith can perceive. Whoever doesn't connect with what can't be seen, out of lack of formation or habit, usually grows very bored. They go to Mass out of obligation and focus on the only thing they do understand: the homily. What a difference there is between

---

24   At the consecration he also tells us, "Drink!" inviting our response (see Mt 20:22; 1 Cor 10:16–33).

25   See *Catechism*, no. 1131.

attending Mass to get together with friends and maybe see your neighbor's new coat, and participating in the Eucharist with an awareness of being present at the most sublime events of the history of salvation!

The Holy Mass is without a doubt the most monumental thing that happens in this world. It's like leaping beyond space and time. It's celebrated on earth, but all heaven participates. Since "time blends with eternity,"[26] attending Holy Mass is "like loosening our ties with earth and time."[27] Every time it is celebrated, the Paschal Mystery is renewed in a way that is unbloody but real and present: it thus becomes the only "event of history which does not pass away . . . all other historical events happen once, and then they pass away, swallowed up in the past . . . . The event of the Cross and Resurrection *abides*."[28] In some sense, by means of a "mysterious 'contemporaneity,' " between what happened two thousand years ago "and the passage of the centuries,"[29] the times are *fused*. In that *memorial of the Passion* the *physical pain* of Jesus on the Cross is present, as well as his *inner pain*, until the end of time.

26   Escrivá, *Christ Is Passing By*, no. 94.
27   Escrivá, *Conversations*, no. 113.
28   *Catechism*, no. 1085.
29   St. John Paul II, Encyclical on the Eucharist in Its Relationship to the Church *Ecclesia de Eucharistia* (April 17, 2003), nos. 59 and 5. Vatican website: www. vatican.va.

In the face of this great mystery, words and explanations fall far short. As St. John Paul II has stated, the Eucharistic doctrine of the Church, despite all the valuable contributions of so many theologians and saints throughout all the centuries, "still reaches no more than the threshold, since it is incapable of grasping and translating into words what the Eucharist is in all its fullness, what is expressed by it and what is actuated by it. Indeed, the Eucharist is the ineffable Sacrament!"[30] Without neglecting the reverent attitude that ought to accompany any reflection on this mystery, perhaps one of the possible keys to continue delving deeper into that inexhaustible reality could be what we have seen regarding the *pain of the Heart of Jesus until the end of time.* We know that mysterious *contemporaneity* exists between the Holy Mass and what happened during the bloody Passion of Christ. Along these same lines, we can speak, too, of a certain *simultaneity,* inasmuch as the Eucharistic sacrifice contains not only the sufferings of Calvary but also the interior sufferings of Christ because of sins, including those that are committed in our own day. Thus, not only the *unified character* of the work of Redemption (see Heb 9:26) but also its *temporal unfolding* *come into focus.*

Each Mass is essentially the same because it contains the same Paschal Mystery. However, since it includes the

---

30   St. John Paul II, *Redemptor Hominis*, no. 20.

immolation of Jesus "in remission of the sins committed daily,"[31] there is something new in it each day: today's Mass is not exactly like the previous one, since between them a small part of the burden caused to the heart of Jesus by sins that continue is consummated. Besides, each Eucharistic celebration, though identical, is numerically distinct. It merges all the redemptive zeal of Christ toward the people of every age, but those in attendance vary: the blessed are always present, as well as the souls in purgatory, but only a portion of those on pilgrimage toward heaven. The redemptive sacrifice is offered for all, but only some participate in it when it is renewed sacramentally on earth, and those can apply it to their intentions. When he instituted the Eucharist, Jesus affirmed that his blood would be poured out *pro vobis et pro multis* (for you and for many), thus distinguishing among the apostles there present and the rest of his beneficiaries.

The intimate relation between the events of that memorable night and those of Good Friday is striking. It becomes obvious that the Holy Mass is a true sacrifice that perpetuates Christ's Passion. The *first Mass in history* began during the Last Supper and ended with Jesus' death on the Cross. While he was celebrating the Passover in the Cenacle, he only drank three of the four cups that the Jewish rite

---

31   See St. Paul VI, Encyclical on the Holy Eucharist *Mysterium Fidei* (September 3, 1965), no. 27. Vatican website: www.vatican.va.

prescribed. He drank the fourth a little before he died: when he agreed to try that cheap wine offered by a compassionate soldier (see Jn 19:28–30).[32] Only then could he confirm that all was finished. The old agreement between us and God was definitively fulfilled, and Jesus became the Passover lamb who sealed with his blood the "new and eternal covenant." The night before, to institute the priesthood and perpetuate that *single Mass of all of history*, Jesus said, "Do this in memory of me." He assured us that he himself would be present in each celebration when, before the supper, he exclaimed, "I have earnestly desired to eat this passover with you before I suffer; for I tell you I shall not eat it until it is fulfilled in the kingdom of God" (Lk 22:15–16).[33]

That *one* Mass begun on Holy Thursday will last until Christ's Second Coming. This is how St. Paul synthesizes the Eucharistic doctrine: "For as often as you eat this bread and drink the cup, you proclaim the Lord's death until he comes" (1 Cor 11:26). When this world comes to an end, the Eucharist will no longer be celebrated. There will no longer be anyone on the way to heaven, and the work of Redemption will have been consummated.

In the meantime, the Holy Mass allows us to be *present* for each of Christ's redemptive sorrows and joys. The

---

32 See also Scott Hahn, *A Father Who Keeps His Promises* (New York: Doubleday, 2007).

33 See also Mt 26:29; Mk 14:25.

consecration is like a window that opens and allows us to *contemplate* past, present, and future events.[34] It's like *being* at once on Golgotha and in heaven, where Jesus "does not cease to offer himself for us."[35] If we participate in the Eucharist with lively faith and ardent love, we'll never recover from our amazement. It is certainly the most stunning thing we can do in this life. Attending Holy Mass is not like seeing a film; it's not even like seeing a rebroadcast: it's equivalent to watching live all the redemptive joys and sufferings of Christ. It's not the same thing *to be transported there* with a distant attitude as with affective harmony. *Living in* the heart of Jesus for only a minute—as long as the consecration lasts— is itself an overpowering experience: in that short lapse of time, some hundred people will die, thousands of sins will be committed, and many joys will be procured. All these things have their echoes in the Sacred Heart.

If we are aware of being present at such sublime events whenever we attend the renewal of the redemptive sacrifice,

34   Immediately after the consecration, the Church's liturgy recalls to us that we are celebrating the memorial of the Paschal Mystery. To break down what's happening, the two most ancient Eucharistic Prayers, 1 and 2, mention the death, Resurrection, and Ascension of Jesus Christ into heaven, while the two more recent ones, 3 and 4, add a passage referring to our waiting in hope for his glorious return. This reference to the Parousia reflects, perhaps, a growing awareness on the part of the Church that in the Holy Mass not only past events, but also, in an equally mysterious manner, future ones are "made present."

35   Roman Missal, Paschal Preface 3.

we won't adopt a passive attitude, nor will we arrive empty-handed. Rather, we will engage personally: during the Offertory, we will put on the paten, beside the bread that will become the Body of Christ, everything we've done to concretize our co-redemptive zeal since the last time we attended Mass.

Generosity in corresponding to the love of Christ is something very intimate for each of us to decide about in the quiet of our own prayer. At bottom, it's a response to the veiled invitation to co-redeem which Jesus addresses to us with the words of the consecration that transform the wine into his Blood: "Take and drink all of you, for this is the chalice of my Blood," he says to each one of us. He is asking us delicately not to leave him alone, to be like Mary, helping him each day to console the Father and save souls. Indeed, in Jewish culture, to "drink from a cup" means to participate actively in the sacrifice (see 1 Cor 10:16–33).[36]

If we respond positively to that loving request, the Holy Mass is transformed into "the center and the source" of our spiritual life:[37] the point in which all our zeal converges with the font of grace that nourishes our soul and strengthens us to be able to imitate Christ. The Mass focuses all our concerns,

36   In Mt 20:22, Jesus asks the two apostles if they wish to drink of the chalice from which he will drink.

37   Escrivá, *Christ Is Passing By*, no. 87. That expression was picked up from *Presbyterorum Ordinis*, no. 14.

united around what should be the most important one of all: relieving the heart of Jesus of its burdens. Each time we unite ourselves to the sacrifice of the altar, our greatest longing becomes reality, and at the same time those words of Jesus from the Cross—*that he would draw* all things to himself (see Jn 12:32)—are verified in us. And like a root that nourishes us, from the Eucharist proceeds the strength we need to overcome any obstacle and transform any adversity into an opportunity to co-redeem with Christ.

When that sublime redemptive zeal inspires our whole struggle, in a perfect *unity of life*, the whole day becomes a Mass. Our actions, united to the holy sacrifice, acquire an incalculable value; our offerings, poor as they may be, participate in the redemptive efficacy of the Cross of Christ, like those simple drops of water which, poured into the wine of the chalice during the Offertory, are transformed first into wine and then, during the consecration, into the Blood.

Our ordinary life thus acquires an extraordinary fruitfulness and transcendence: in the midst of our little daily ups and downs, placing love into the duty of each instant, we contribute to "unite all things in [Christ]" (Eph 1:10). Could there be anything grander than collaborating so closely with the Redemption of the human race, lightening the Cross of our Lord Jesus Christ while also helping him to console God the Father and obtain the grace of the Holy Spirit, which makes possible the salvation of millions of people?

This union with the Eucharistic sacrifice allows us to exercise a *common priesthood*, a logical consequence of our being configured to Christ by our baptism.[38] It translates into seeking to live with a *priestly soul*, a fundamental attitude that emerges from our identification with the ardent redemptive sentiments of the heart of Jesus, and which spurs us on to transform our entire existence into an occasion of co-redeeming with Christ. Thus, this "holy priesthood," to which St. Peter refers (1 Pt 2:5), doesn't distance us from our occupations in the middle of the world. Rather, they lead us to make of them "spiritual sacrifices acceptable to God through Jesus Christ" (1 Pt 2:5). Indeed, through the Holy Mass, each one of us, as we offer Christ (to the Father for all souls), offer ourselves with him.

---

38 Essentially distinct from the *common priesthood of the faithful* (and not only in degree), in the *ministerial priesthood of the clergy*, those who are able to receive the Sacrament of Holy Orders to "act as a representative of Christ, Head of the Church" (*Catechism*, no. 1581), especially when they lend their voice to pronounce the words of consecration and absolution of sins. We will never be able to be sufficiently grateful for that priesthood. If it didn't exist, our spiritual impoverishment would be tremendous: we wouldn't be able to be sure our sins had been forgiven, we wouldn't have Jesus in the tabernacle, and although he would still be offering himself to the Father for us, we wouldn't be able to be sacramentally *present* at that redemptive sacrifice, nor would we be able to "materialize" our co-redemptive offering, nor have its fruits available to us (or apply them for the benefit of particular people, or receive Holy Communion ourselves).

Being in tune with Jesus Christ, the High and Eternal Priest, fosters in us both the desire to *console the Father* and to *save all souls*. Let's reflect on this second aspect now: *heaven for souls*. It's not possible for us to share the zeal for his heart and not sacrifice ourselves, day after day, gladly, with the aim of easing the eternal salvation of any human being. Nothing brings greater joy to our Lord than when people, overcoming their hesitation, decide to open themselves to his love.

In some sense, as mediators in Christ, we "represent" each one of our brothers and sisters: we are their "backers" before God. Thus it is that no one, living or dead, leaves us indifferent. From among the three hundred billion deceased people, we will feel the urge to help those who, already sure of their eternal salvation, are on the path to purification and sanctification, in order to be able to enter heaven. Thus, a relationship of friendship is opened up with all those *souls in purgatory* which, in their turn, manifest their gratitude by interceding for us.

As for the living, our priestly soul presses us on to concrete apostolic action, above all in the form of a *personal apostolate* which consists of helping each of our acquaintances to draw closer to God. With the example and well-timed words of a good friend, we'll help them see that living as a Christian is worthwhile. We'll tell them, in confidence, how much Jesus loves them and how much he suffers when they reject that love. Only God can change hearts, but he sends us as instruments in his hands. He wants to do it by means of us, because in that way he respects their freedom more fully: it's easier to say no to the "messenger" than to the "sender," in person. In that zeal for souls, the particular lives alongside the universal. This is why, at each Mass, besides commending our relatives and friends, it's urgent to offer ourselves up for the person and intentions of the Holy Father and for the conversion of every unrepentant sinner. In a special way, let's pray daily for those who are dying and, among them, those who will not be saved unless they change their stance on that last day of their life.

The time has come to bring these pages to an end. St. Josemaría is the one who has taught us the most about our co-redemption with Christ through the Eucharist. These words of his are a fine summary of everything we've seen here.

In the Holy Mass we find the perfect opportunity to expiate our own sins and those of all men: to be able to say, with St. Paul, that we are completing in our flesh what is lacking in the sufferings of Christ. No one is alone in the world; no one can consider himself free of part of the blame in the evil that is committed on earth, a consequence of original sin and also of the sum of many personal sins. Let us love sacrifice; let us seek expiation. How? By joining ourselves in the Holy Mass to Christ, Priest and Victim: it will always be he who carries the imposing weight of the infidelities of his creatures, of yours and mine.[39]

If we feel crushed by our unworthiness to participate in such an exalted mystery, let's allow Mary to purify our offerings. Let us offer everything to the Lord through her. Let us have recourse with all trust to her who is the Co-redemptrix *par excellence*, to be able to associate ourselves more closely each day to the Cross of her Son. This ancient prayer, which some are accustomed to reciting privately during the consecration at Mass, is a fine summary of everything we've seen here: "Holy Father, through the Immaculate Heart of Mary, I offer you Jesus, your most beloved Son, and I offer myself in him, through him, and with him, for all his intentions, in the name of all Christians."

With gratitude before such magnificence, the only thing left to add is "Blessed are those who are invited to the marriage supper of the Lamb" (Rv 19:9).

---

39   As quoted in Ernesto Juliá, *El santo de lo ordinario* (Alicante: Cobel, 2010), p. 149.